THE JOBS ACT

CROWDFUNDING FOR SMALL BUSINESSES AND STARTUPS

———————————

William Michael Cunningham

The JOBS Act: Crowdfunding for Small Businesses and Startups

ISBN-13 (pbk): 978-1-4302-4755-5
ISBN-13 (electronic): 978-1-4302-4756-2

Trademarked names may appear in this book. Rather than use a trademark symbol with every occurrence of a trademarked name, we use the names only in an editorial fashion and to the benefit of the trademark owner, with no intention of infringement of the trademark.

President and Publisher: Paul Manning
Lead Editor: Jeff Olson
Editorial Board: Steve Anglin, Mark Beckner, Ewan Buckingham, Gary Cornell, Louise Corrigan, Morgan Ertel, Jonathan Gennick, Jonathan Hassell, Robert Hutchinson, Michelle Lowman, James Markham, Matthew Moodie, Jeff Olson, Jeffrey Pepper, Douglas Pundick, Ben Renow-Clarke, Dominic Shakeshaft, Gwenan Spearing, Matt Wade, Tom Welsh
Coordinating Editor: Rita Fernando
Copy Editor: Terry Kornak
Compositor: Bytheway Publishing Services
Indexer: SPi Global
Cover Designer: Anna Ishchenko

Distributed to the book trade worldwide by Springer-Verlag New York, Inc., 233 Spring Street, 6th Floor, New York, NY 10013. Phone 1-800-SPRINGER, fax 201-348-4505, e-mail orders-ny@springer-sbm.com, or visit www.springeronline.com.

For information on translations, please contact us by e-mail at info@apress.com, or visit www.apress.com.

Apress and friends of ED books may be purchased in bulk for academic, corporate, or promotional use. eBook versions and licenses are also available for most titles. For more information, reference our Special Bulk Sales–eBook Licensing web page at www.apress.com/bulk-sales. To place an order, e-mail your request to support@apress.com

FOR MY MOTHER

Contents

About the Author

William Michael Cunningham is an economist, investment advisor, researcher, and social investing policy analyst. Cunningham researches, evaluates, develops, and creates specific socially responsible investments. On February 6, 2006, he warned the SEC that statistical models he created using his Fully Adjusted Return Methodology signaled the possibility of system-wide economic and market failure. A former securities broker and institutional salesman, he works with pension fund trustees, investment managers, community activists, government agencies, and financial industry organizations to create and implement social and community investing initiatives. Cunningham has testified before the Ways and Means and Financial Services Committees of the U.S. House of Representatives. In an October 1998 petition to the United States Court of Appeals, he opposed the elimination of the Glass–Steagall Act, citing evidence that growing financial market malfeasance greatly reduced the safety and integrity of large financial institutions. Cunningham has been involved in the provision of online resources to small businesses for more than 15 years, posting his first website in 1995. In 2002, he created a proposal for an early version of crowdfunding. Cunningham holds an MA in economics from the University of Chicago, as well as an MBA in finance from the university's Booth School of Business.

Acknowledgments

I thank my college and graduate school interns, current and former, for their help. They are a remarkable group of talented young people. I have been honored to work with all of them.

In the current year, Mr. Thilina Basnayake, a second-year student at the University of Virginia, has been extremely helpful. He worked on this book as part of his summer internship with Creative Investment Research, Inc.

I also thank Claiborne Booker, an alumnus of the Booth School at the University of Chicago and Creative Investment Research, Inc., Advisory Board member Larry McCoy. Both were a great help, as was American Legion Kenneth H. Nash Post 8.

Last, but not least, Lineage Family Reunion members Gladys and William David Jackson were instrumental in providing needed assistance that allowed me to complete this book so quickly.

Introduction

Social media is one of the most remarkable developments of the Internet revolution. One need look no further than Egypt, the United Kingdom, the United States, Syria, or Libya to view the influence that online communities have had in the political sphere. Now, this power has come to the business world, specifically the marketplace for equity shares in business startups.

On April 5, 2012, President Obama signed the Jumpstart Our Business Startups Act, better known as the JOBS Act. The Act is designed to "reopen American capital markets to small companies," defined as "emerging growth companies." I believe this is one of the most significant legislative initiatives since the Securities and Exchange Acts of 1933 and 1934. This law changes everything.

A composite of several pieces of proposed legislation,[1] the final version of the JOBS Act, H.R. 3606, was passed by the House of Representatives on March 7, 2012. The Senate passed its version of the legislation on March 22, 2012. Supporters included the National Venture Capital Association, the Small Business and Entrepreneurship Council, the National Small Business Association, the U.S. Chamber of Commerce, the International Franchise Association, and the Biotechnology Industry Organization. Crowdfunding platform Indiegogo also supported the law. Opponents included the American Association of Retired Persons and the North American Securities Administrators Association. The owner of crowdfunding platform Kickstarter has indicated that his firm is "not gearing up for the equity wave if it comes.[2]"

Small businesses and startups can now raise up to $1 million in equity (or debt) funding online via what are called "Crowdfunding Platforms"—online communities and websites. Imagine an eBay-like site that allows you to post your idea for a commercial venture online and then allows investors to

---

[1] H.R. 2930, H.R. 2940, H.R. 1070, H.R. 2167, H.R. 3606, H.R. 4088.

[2] Om Malik, "Kickstarted: My Conversation with Kickstarter Co-founder Perry Chen," May 22, 2012. GigaOM. Available at: http://gigaom.com/2012/05/22/kickstarter-founder-perry-chen-intervie/

purchase equity shares or stakes in it. As one journalist put it, it's social media meets venture capital.

I believe that not only will companies now be able to use the Internet to raise significant amounts of capital (equity or debt) funding but, having done so, they will also use the new media to drive in new ways sales, product development, distribution, social/sustainability benefits, compliance/branding issues, and customer support. This really changes everything. This book is about the development and implementation of the law, what it means, and how and why it will impact the business startup marketplace. The book also describes significant transformational opportunities, and risks, for those seeking to understand the economic implications of the new law.

Not just for entrepreneurs, the book will benefit securities lawyers, community development specialists, educators, venture capitalists, and those offering services in the new crowdfunding arena. It is, simply, the most current and most comprehensive compendium of information on the law and its impact on this new market.

Plan of the Book

I start at the beginning, with a summary of the JOBS Act. Next, I review the current financing environment for startups, followed by a review of Emerging Growth Companies (EGCs), a new business firm category created by the JOBS Act. I cover disclosure and crowdfunding in the next chapters. Portals, like Indiegogo and Kickstarter, are described next. I end where we began, with a section by section review of the JOBS Act.

Important note: Many details of the law still need to be worked out, and the SEC is working on rules and regulations on how the JOBS Act will play out in the real world. My website, www.minorityfinance.com, will contain a rundown of the rules as they come out.

It's essential you are fully up to date with the regulations before you even think about raising money via crowdfunding. The laws may have eased when it comes to raising capital for your company, but that doesn't mean they are easy. You can still pay significant penalties for making mistakes when offering securities.

Summary of the JOBS Act

The JOBS Act represents a fundamental change in the business financing environment. Many companies, previously blocked out of the market for capital, will now be able to obtain business financing. This will lead to disruptions across the board.

The JOBS Act starts by encouraging small companies to sell stock to the public (known as "going public"). The second section of the law eliminates certain restrictions against selling stock to the general public, lowering certain outdated safeguards meant to prevent the sale of securities to persons and institutions who are unqualified or unprepared to purchase them.

The third section of the law, the crowdfunding provision, targets emerging growth companies and defines them as an equity security issuer with "total annual gross revenues of less than $1,000,000,000 . . . during its most recently completed fiscal year." These firms are now exempt from certain reporting requirements, making it easier to raise capital. As you'll see, this is a big deal.

Here's what makes up Part I.

Chapter 1: The JOBS Act: Summary and Definitions

To understand the law and take advantage of it, you must know the precise meaning of several terms, including *emerging growth company* and *crowdfunding*.

In addition, you must understand the set of institutional arrangements that govern the market for startup financing. Using examples, charts, and graphs, I describe the marketplace dominated by emerging growth companies.

Chapter 2: Startup Financing Environment: Why the JOBS Act Now?

Using information on startup business capital flows, I describe how startups are currently financed, the impact of the financial crisis on the availability of capital for startup businesses, and how the JOBS Act will improve financing opportunities for small companies.

Chapter 3: Emerging Growth Companies: Facts, Figures, and Potential

Chapter 3 provides baseline information on emerging growth companies (EGCs), companies with less than $1 billion in revenue. I list the number of EGCs in each state, the number of EGCs in each industry, and compare the entrepreneurial environment in the United States with that in China. Finally, I describe how the JOBS Act will impact this sector.

The JOBS Act
Summary and Definitions

The JOBS Act (Jumpstart Our Business Startups Act) is a revolutionary development in the world of startup and small business financing. Among other things, for the first time, startups and small businesses can use the power of the Internet to raise equity capital from investors across the country and around the globe. The act allows small companies, including startups, to raise, via crowdfunding (described later), up to $1 million per year, subject to five-year time limit, along with a $700 million market-value limit. For such companies, the act has also created exemptions to accounting and auditing rules, as well as to rules that require public companies to report details concerning executive compensation and other financial data.

All of this has the potential to be a very good deal for startup and small businesses. The aim of this book is to look at the details of the JOBS Act and not only show you what's happening from the 40,000-foot level, but also provide a ground-level interpretive and helpful review of the act, a review you can use to obtain capital to start or fund an existing firm, or help others do so. It should also prove helpful to investors looking for opportunities to invest in promising companies on an equal footing with other investors.

To start, the JOBS Act targets Emerging Growth Companies (EGCs) and defines them as companies that:

1. Are issuing stock or equity and

2. Have annual receipts or revenues of less than $1 billion in their most recent fiscal year.

Table 1-1 summarizes the main points of the law.

Table 1-1. Summary of the JOBS Act

The JOBS Act: Public Law 112-106, House Bill Number H.R. 3606, Signed into Law on April 5, 2012
Title I: Reopening American Capital Markets to Emerging Growth Companies
Defines "Emerging Growth Company" (EGC): Firm with less than $1 billion in revenue and first sale of common equity after 12/8/11.
Exempts EGCs from executive compensation shareholder approval requirement.
Exempts EGCs from needing to present more than two years of audited financial statements.
Exempts EGCs from compliance with any new or revised financial accounting standards, with certain limits.
Exempts EGCs from audit and attestation requirement concerning internal controls, with certain limits.
Exempts EGCs from compliance with auditing or other Public Company Accounting Oversight Board (PCAOB) accounting standards.
Exempts broker/dealers from pre-offering reports on EGCs.
Prohibits Securities Exchange Commission (SEC) or national securities associations from applying conflict-of-interest rules or regulations concerning an Initial Public Offering (IPO) of an EGC.
Allows an EGC to solicit qualified institutional buyers or accredited investors.
Prohibits SEC or national securities associations from applying rules or regulations concerning the publication of research reports on EGCs.
Allows an EGC to submit a confidential draft registration statement to the SEC.
Requires the SEC to study "decimalization," a system that allows security prices to be given in one-penny ($0.01) increments.
Allows an EGC to forgo exemptions granted under the act.
Requires the SEC to study modernizing Regulation S-K. Regulation S-K establishes certain reporting requirements, rules that govern which data must be reported to investors, and when.

Title II: Access to Capital for Job Creators

Requires the SEC to modify Regulation D so that general solicitation and advertising prohibitions do not apply if all buyers are accredited investors. Regulation D, according to the U.S. Securities and Exchange Commission (the SEC), is a regulation containing "three rules providing exemptions from (security offering) registration requirements, allowing some companies to sell their securities without having to register the securities with the SEC."[1]

Requires issuers to verify security buyers are accredited.

Mandates that the SEC allow security sales, under this exemption, to those the seller believes are qualified institutional buyers.

Mandates that Regulation D–exempt offerings do not become public offerings "as a result of general advertising or general solicitation."

Exempts certain persons from broker/dealer registration under three conditions.

Title III: Crowdfunding

Defines terms under which transactions of $1 million or less are exempt from certain registration requirements. Crowdfunding is raising equity capital funds for a startup or small business firm from a relatively large number of small investors.

Defines a "funding portal."

Defines requirements for a crowdfunding exemption.

Defines exemption from shareholder caps.

Defines funding portal exemption, portal SEC, and national security association examination dependency. (In other words, portals are exempt from certain SEC registration rules, but are required to remain subject to examination by the SEC and other regulators.)

Does not allow a state or any governmental subdivision to enforce laws or initiate certain actions against funding portals, subject to limits. (These limits are described in later sections of the book.)

Title IV: Small Company Capital Formation

Directs the SEC to exempt certain small companies from Regulation A, a class of securities with less than $50 million in aggregate offerings over a 12-month period. This limit was increased from $5 million.

Mandates that securities covered by the exemption be equity, debt, or debt securities convertible to equity.

Describes disclosure, reporting, electronic filing, disclosure termination, and exemption disqualification requirements.
Mandates a biannual review of the $50 million dollar limit.
Releases securities covered by the section from state regulation.
Mandates "Blue-Sky" study. "Blue-Sky" laws are state laws governing the sale and offering of securities.
Title V: Private Company Flexibility and Growth
Increases shareholder registration requirement to $10 million from $1 million for issuers with either 2,000 "shareholders of record" or 500 accredited investors.
Exempts securities received as part of employee compensation from held of record calculation.
Title VI: Capital Expansion
Increases shareholder registration requirement to $10 million from $1 million for issuers with 2,000 shareholders of record for a bank or bank holding company.
Mandates termination of registration if number of shareholders of record falls below 1,200 for a bank or bank holding company.
Title VII: Outreach on Changes to the Law
Requires the SEC notify small and medium-sized, women-owned, veteran, and minority-owned businesses of changes made by the act.

I explain most of these important changes in securities laws in the rest of the book. But the bottom line is that small businesses will now find it easier to raise capital. Let's take a look at some of the more important pieces of the legislation.

Increased Capital-Raising Allowances

The JOBS Act increases the amount of money that can be raised using standard exemptions to the securities registration and reporting requirements, and it allows startups and small companies to raise capital over the Internet. At its best, the law recognizes that changes in technology have necessitated a revision to securities laws. Figures 1-1 and 1-2 place the changes in context.

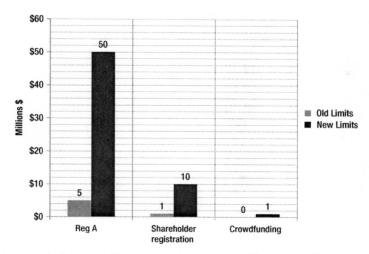

Figure 1-1. Changes to capital-raising limits as a result of the JOBS Act.

Figure 1-1 shows how the act changes the amount of money that can be raised via small company offerings and crowdfunding. The revision to small company offering limits (Reg A in the chart, short for Regulation A) are significant, growing from $5 to $50 million. Crowdfunding, however, moves from zero to $1 million, a percentage increase of, well, infinity. The crowdfunding dollar amount allowed is 50 times smaller than the Reg A limit. Hopefully this provides some context. While the change is significant, the dollar amount allowed via crowdfunding is well below that of other security offering options.

In addition to allowing new forms of capital access, the law also increases the number of shareholders needed to trip what is known as the shareholder trigger, the point at which a company must register its securities with the SEC. Figure 1-2 shows the old and the new triggers in general (Public Company SOR Trigger) and for banks and for bank holding companies (B, BHC SOR Trigger).

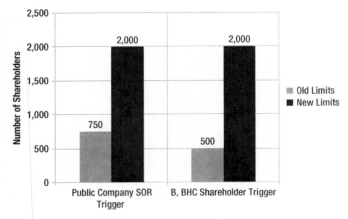

Figure 1-2. Change in number of shareholders needed to trigger SEC reporting requirements. B = Bank; BHC = Bank Holding Company; SOR = Shareholder of Record.

Exemptions from Certain Reporting Requirements

EGCs seeking debt or equity funding are now exempt from a number of requirements regarding the reporting of certain financial data. These reporting requirements were enshrined in the Securities and Exchange Acts of 1933 and 1934, and they have governed the rules for raising equity capital ever since, so this is a big change. Firms that issued stock on or before December 8, 2011 are not covered by the act, however.

According to the law, EGCs *do not* need to:

1. "Present more than 2 years of audited financial statements in order for the registration statement of such emerging growth company with respect to an initial public offering of its common equity securities to be effective."

2. "Comply with any new or revised financial accounting standard as defined under section 2(a) of the Sarbanes-Oxley Act of 2002 (15 U.S.C. 7201(a))."

Further, broker/dealers are exempt from restrictions concerning the publication or distribution of research reports about an EGC's stock. These research reports are not considered an offer to sell securities, an important exemption. In the language of the law, these research reports published will "not . . . constitute an offer for sale or offer to sell a security, even if the broker or dealer is participating or will participate in the registered offering of the securities of the issuer."

The act loosens rules concerning sales, solicitation, reporting, and accounting that discourage many startup and small companies from going public. In addition, investment banks and brokers are free to publish and distribute research reports on small and startup companies without worrying that they will conflict with SEC rules and regulations.

Furthermore, there is no "quiet period" for these EGC issuers. Previously, from the time a company submitted and filed with the SEC a formal notice that it was raising equity, known as a registration statement, to the point at which staff at the SEC determined that the registration statement was legal, issuers could say only a limited number of things to the public about what they were doing. This new law allows EGCs to speak to the public about what they are doing and why they are raising capital. Given the nature of Internet technology, this only makes sense. More on this later.

Further, the JOBS Act limits the ability of the SEC to restrict communications between a securities analyst and a potential investor based on the analyst's role in an EGC's stock offering. The SEC cannot restrict an analyst's ability to participate in telephone calls, e-mails, conference calls, or any other communication. These exclusions cover the management of an EGC and persons working for or with a securities firm or securities association.

The law states that the EGC or persons "authorized to act on behalf of an emerging growth company" can communicate, verbally or otherwise, with potential investors that are "qualified institutional buyers or institutions that are accredited investors.[1]"

Finally, the act directs the SEC to revise its rules "to provide that the prohibition against general solicitation or general advertising . . . shall not apply to offers and sales of (emerging company) securities . . . provided that all purchasers of the securities are accredited investors."

Funding Portals

As noted earlier, crowdfunding can be defined as the process of raising equity, or ownership capital for a startup or small business firm from a relatively large number of small investors.

---

[1] An "accredited" investor is an individual with a high net worth and thus deemed to be sophisticated when it comes to financial matters.

Funding portals are websites used to facilitate the flow of capital from investors to crowdfunded EGCs. They are central to the crowdfunding process. Those providing a platform for the sale of EGC securities do not need to register with the SEC as a broker/dealer, provided they meet certain conditions:

1. Even if a funding platform does not register with the SEC as a broker/ dealer, it will still be required to register with the SEC. It will also be subject to the SEC's "examination, enforcement, and other rulemaking authority."

2. If a platform does not register as a broker/dealer with the SEC, then it cannot receive any "compensation in connection with the purchase or sale of" EGC securities and cannot have "possession of customer funds or securities."

3. If a platform does not register as a broker/dealer with the SEC, then it cannot be compensated for providing investment advice concerning the EGC securities on its own or other EGC portal websites.

These rules are an effort by Congress to both protect investors and provide incentives for those seeking to serve as intermediaries—those who connect the startups and small businesses needing capital with those with money to invest. As long as you do not control customer money and do not recommend companies on your crowdfunding website, you can avoid the complicated and restrictive rules that govern firms selling securities in the general marketplace. To protect investors, you will still need to let the SEC know who you are, however.

■ **Note**   While this sounds like the law is structured so that funding platforms cannot make money, we think two things are going on here. First, the law pushes platforms to register as broker/dealers, providing another advantage to an industry that may not deserve it. Second, there will be unregistered funding platforms. They will figure out a way to make money. We just don't know how, yet.

Portal Requirements

Funding platforms must register with the SEC as a broker or as a funding portal. They must also register with one or more self-regulatory organizations, like Financial Industry Regulatory Authority (FINRA) or another regulatory agency. Funding portals must also disclose EGC stock and security risks and provide "other investor education materials."

Portals must take responsibility for training investors, a new requirement that fits well with this marketplace, given the heightened risk of investing in small firms. Portals will use new social media tools to fulfill this obligation. This will be a major factor in this marketplace.

To the extent that a startup or small firm creates a product or service that uniquely addresses a real market need, both customers and investors will take notice. Social media, like YouTube, Facebook, and LinkedIn, will amplify this information. These potential network effects could be significant. If word gets out about a breakthrough product or service, it might be possible to raise significant amounts of money far faster than before. Likewise, there is also the risk that investors can lose money quickly. I am betting on the former, however, and I believe that "the wisdom of the crowd" will serve to limit outright fraud. I expect to see a number of YouTube crowdfunding channels, crowdfunding pages on Facebook and LinkedIn, in-person seminars and webinars, and other efforts to educate crowdfunding investors. This effort will have the added benefit of teaching people about investing in general. Financial literacy in the United States may improve.

Portals must do more than provide information on small company investing. They must also certify that each crowdfunding investor using their platforms has reviewed and understands information on the risk of investing in small firms. The portals must affirm "that the (EGC) investor understands that the investor is risking the loss of the entire investment, and that the investor could bear such a loss." They must, according to the law, make sure investors have:

1. An understanding of the level of risk generally applicable to investments in startups, emerging businesses, and small issuers;

2. An understanding of the risk of illiquidity; and

3. An understanding of such other matters as the Commission determines appropriate, by rule.

Investment Restrictions

The law is clear about how much and from whom you can raise the money when you use crowdfunding portals. EGCs, for example, are limited to raising $1 million in any 12-month period. Individual investors can only spend the greater of $2,000 or 5% of their net income, if their net income is less than

$100,000, on crowdfunded shares. If they have a net worth greater than $100,000, they can spend 10% of their net income on the stocks and securities of EGCs, up to a "maximum aggregate amount sold of $100,000." So, if your income is $1 million, 10% of this would be $100,000. This is what you can spend on Crowdfunded securities, the same amount you can spend if your income is $5 million.

This is an extremely important change to securities laws. You no longer need to be an "accredited"—high net worth—investor to get in on ground-floor opportunities to buy into startups. The law thus opens the door to regular citizens seeking to make investments in startup and small companies, a door that was previously only open to people with a lot of money. The JOBS Act does this while protecting small, moderate-income investors by limiting the amount of money they can put into these small, new, and relatively risky firms.

Small Company Risk

Potential investors in EGCs must understand something clearly: Small companies go out of business with great regularity. There is no guarantee that crowdfunding investors will see a return on their money. They need to understand that they could lose their entire investment. In addition, even if they do not lose their money, they may not be able to access it for some time. This is called liquidity risk—the risk that you may not be able to get your money back when you need it.

Other risks will become apparent only after this market gets going, and the SEC will require portals to educate potential investors about them.

Fraud Prevention

Funding portals must be concerned with fraud. They will publish background information on portal owners and on issuers. This information will include data on violations of security market regulations, if any, committed by those seeking crowdfunding.

■ **Note**   Authenticity Matters: in one case on a donations based (not equity) crowdfunding portal, a family-owned business sought funding donations to save the firm. It turns out that this family had run several other businesses into the ground. The crowd sniffed this out and rejected the campaign.

Twenty-One-Day Dissemination and Goal Meeting

No later than 21 days after the first day on which EGC securities are sold, funding portals must "make available to the Securities and Exchange Commission and to potential investors any information provided by the issuer."

Moreover, funding portals can, by law, provide funds raised to EGCs only when they meet their fundraising goal or target, or, in the words of the law, "when the aggregate capital raised from all investors is equal to or greater than a target offering amount." Portals must also "allow all investors to cancel their commitments to invest"—to back out if they get cold feet.

EGCs thus get funds raised only if they meet or exceed their funding target. How might this work?

Let's say your restaurant seeks to take advantage of a temporary opportunity, for example, the fact that the Super Bowl is coming to your town. You need $100,000 for a new storefront and equipment. You believe that, by getting ready now, you will significantly increase the amount of money your restaurant makes. You are willing to sell part of your restaurant operation to outsiders in exchange for the money you need. By launching a successful crowdfunding campaign, one that raises at least $100,000, you get the money you need. This might work by selling ownership shares in your restaurant for $10.00 each.

If you get commitments for only $90,000, the deal is off and you have to go home and lick your wounds. But if you get $100,000 or more, you get your funding and start work on renovating your restaurant.

A year later, when the Super Bowl is in town, you discover that your hunch was correct: your receipts are up by 50% because you are selling many more meals. Investors know this fact because you must provide them regular financial reports, probably via the funding portal on which you initially sold shares. Other small company investors read these financial reports and bid up the price from $10 a share to $20. They buy them from your original crowdfunding investors. Who benefits? You are better off because you got low-cost financing to take advantage of an opportunity. Your original investors doubled their money. Your new investors believe you can do even better in the future. Everyone is better off.

Funding portals have an affirmative obligation to make sure that EGC investors abide by certain rules. Funding portals must make sure "that no investor in a 12-month period has purchased securities that, in the aggregate, from all issuers, exceed the investment limits set forth in (the Act)." Moreover, as mentioned earlier, portals must vet investors to ensure they have the income required to invest in what are by nature risky ventures.

This is an area of new activity. It remains to be seen how well portals will monitor EGCs, but, given what's at stake, we have no doubt they will figure it out.

■ **Note** How will funding portals know if you have gone over the income/net worth limits in investing in EGCs? It's not clear, but enterprising crowdfunding portals will soon devise a means.

Privacy Issues

Funding portals must protect the privacy of information obtained from investors using their platform. While these steps are not enumerated in the law, I expect most funding portals will follow standard Internet privacy protocols. These protocols describe what personal information is collected, how it is used, how long it is kept, how it is protected from others, and how consumers can review and, if need be, delete or dispute it. To further protect privacy, portals cannot pay for leads or "compensate promoters, finders, or lead generators for providing the broker or funding portal with the personal identifying information of any potential investor." This means portals cannot pay for e-mail lists or other types of lists.

The purpose behind this part of the law is to stop a potential spam issue. Let's say you are an investor and join a portal. You make a few small investments. This section of the law means that third parties cannot obtain that information and sell it to another portal or to an EGC. Were they able to do so, you would see a lot more junk e-mail in your inbox.

Conflict-of-Interest Prohibition

The law prohibits EGC insiders, such as "directors, officers, or partners (or any person occupying a similar status or performing a similar function) from having any financial interest in an issuer using its services." In other words, EGCs cannot create raise funds through a self-created, self-directed funding portal. You can't create a funding portal just to raise money for your firm.

Requirements for Issuers

The crowdfunding portion of the law provides that EGCs must provide a full set of information to investors, funding portals, and the SEC. In addition to their physical address, EGCs must report detailed information on the current set of officers and board members; provide information on anybody with a significant ownership interest, defined here as greater that 20%; describe how the funds raised will be put to use; and provide either an income tax return, a CPA-prepared financial statement, or a set of fully audited financial statements.

In addition, EGCs must provide information on the price of the securities being offered; the terms (price, structure of the deal, etc.); and the legal and other conditions and rules that impact these ownership stakes. EGCs must describe how investors might be impacted by changes in the ownership structure, including how much of the firm they are buying and the conditions under which that ownership interest may change. They must also detail the risks involved in purchasing shares in the company.

All this protects investors from changes that might significantly and unfairly reduce their share of ownership in an EGC.

Crowdfunding Regulations

The law provides that:

- Issuers cannot "advertise the terms of the (EGC) offering, except for notices which direct investors to the funding portal or broker."

- Issuers cannot compensate, directly or indirectly, persons for promoting security offerings if those persons use a communication channel provided by a "broker or funding portal" unless they disclose this arrangement is in a manner consistent with SEC rules.

- Issuers must "ensure that such person clearly discloses the receipt, past or prospective, of such compensation, upon each instance of such promotional communication."

- Issuers must file an annual report with the Commission. These annual reports go to investors and must "provide to investors reports of the results of operations and financial statements of the issuer, as the Commission shall, by rule, determine appropriate."

- Issuers must comply with other yet to be determined SEC rules "for the protection of investors and in the public interest."

These are rules to protect investors. In short, the law seeks to centralize the distribution of final information on EGC offerings to the portal on which they reside. Methods used to generate interest in an EGC offering are limited and issuers must disclose any compensation paid. On an annual basis, portals have to describe their operations in detail.

EGCs are liable for the amount paid for the security or for damages if the issuer lies about the company or makes a statement that can be regarded as "untrue." If EGCs neglect to mention something that they should have, like any information investors need to determine with accuracy the value of an EGC and the chance that the EGC will do well, the EGC will have to pay investors back.

Trading Restrictions on Crowdfunded Securities

Securities "may not be transferred by the purchaser of such secureties during the 1-year period beginning on the date of purchase, unless such securities are transferred—

A. To the issuer of the securities;

B. To an accredited investor;

C. As part of an offering registered with the Commission; or

D. To a member of the family of the purchaser or the equivalent, or in connection with the death or divorce of the purchaser or other similar circumstance, in the discretion of the Commission."

You are exempt from the trading restriction if you are:

1. On tribal territory or other lands not subject to state or federal law;

2. Subject to SEC reporting requirements;

3. An investment company.

The buyer must hold EGC securities and shares for a year, unless there are special circumstances that make this unwarranted. This is to prevent manipulation and flipping. If I buy shares in an EGC and "pump up" the EGC by posting untrue or exaggerated information of the EGC's prospects on Facebook, the price for the EGC share would, in all likelihood, increase. I might be able to sell my shares right away, before other potential EGC investors can determine the validity of the information I posted. To prevent this, EGC shares cannot be traded to the public for one year after the purchase date.

What this says is that when you buy into an EGC via crowdfunding, you are going to be locked into that investment for at least one year, so be careful.

Note   Buying shares of an EGC through a crowdfunding portal means (with a few exceptions) that you'll need to hold the securities for at least one year before selling them.

In addition, the law states that the SEC must make a special effort to reach out to firms owned by women, veterans, and members of minority groups with information about crowdfunding and other elements of the JOBS Act. Crowdfunding can potentially level the playing field for all small businesses, opening new sources of business capital and revenue for women- and minority-owned firms. Such firms now have an opportunity to raise funds from a wide community of investors, some of whom are specifically interested in helping women and minority firms. This means these firms do not have to go through banks and other financial institutions that have in the past put roadblocks in their way.

While this is no panacea, crowdfunding expands business financing options far wider than before. It's an option more minority- and women-owned firms should consider.

Important Definitions

To understand the JOBS Act, it is important to understand the terms used throughout the book.

First among these is **Emerging Growth Company (EGC)**, defined as a company or entity with less than $1 billion in gross revenue during its most recently completed fiscal year. The technical definition indexes this amount to inflation, so that, for example, what was worth a billion in 2012 was worth only $935,754,177.80 in 2008, calculated using the Consumer Price Index, an index that tracks how much more (or less) things cost over a month. In any case, the $1 billion figure will change slightly each year, depending on the rate of inflation.

Once designated an EGC, a firm must remain one until one of four dates:

- The last day of the fiscal year in which revenues exceed $1 billion;

- The last day of the fiscal year following the fifth anniversary of the first sale on securities;

- The date on which an EGC issues more that $1 billion in nonconvertible debt;

- The date on which the issuer is deemed a large accelerated filer.

Let's look at some other important definitions, in alphabetical order.

Audited financial statement is a listing of company data showing what a firm owns (assets), what it owes (liabilities), and what it spent (expenses), and whether it made or lost (income) in a given time period, most likely three or twelve months. An audited statement is a set of listings that have been reviewed by a third party, typically a Certified Public Accountant (CPA).

Broker/dealer is a firm that legally engages in the sale, transfer, and trading of financial securities. Broker/dealers must register with the SEC and adhere to strict regulatory standards.

Commission is short for the U.S. Securities and Exchange Commission (SEC).

Company is a collection of assets, both money and people, who associate in order to make money, in most cases by providing a good or a service. Companies are formed to carry out a specified task or tasks.

Crowdfunding is a form of financing whereby people purchase equity securities, or ownership stakes, issued by a firm. The term also describes a form of raising money for business and product development whereby people make donations or contributions to the firm. People also crowdfund through product or service purchases. All methods have in common one thing: they provide resources to a new or existing product, service, firm, or company. This financing can take the form of equity, debt, or hybrid securities, and they may be completed using an internet platform to handle the distribution of information, or not.

Debt refers to loans made to a person or company.

Equity refers to an ownership stake in a company.

Financial Industry Regulatory Authority (FINRA) is a financial and investing market self-regulatory organization.

Funding platform is the same as funding portal, but may refer to the underlying technology.

Funding portal is a website that facilitates the provision of capital or other resources to EGC firms.

Initial Public Offering (IPO) is "common equity" or common stock sold by an issuer under an SEC Act of 1933 registration that has been reviewed by the SEC and approved. An IPO is the first time a company has sold ownership stakes to the public. Typically, newer, younger companies issue IPOs. A privately held company can also issue stock, thereby becoming "publicly held." An investment bank or broker/dealer typically helps the firm issue stock by making recommendations concerning the type of security issued, the best time to issue it, and the price the IPO security is likely to fetch in the open market. An IPO is referred to as a "public offering."[2]

Initial Public Offering Date refers to the first date on which "common equity" or common stock is sold by an issuer under an effective SEC Act of 1933 registration.

Reporting requirement is the obligation firms have to provide certain financial data.

Research reports are compilations of information and data concerning a company; issue; industry; federal, state, or local government entity; or other information used to facilitate security purchase and sale decisions. Research reports are typically issued by broker/dealers or investment banks.

Sarbanes-Oxley Act of 2002, also called the Public Company Accounting Reform and Investor Protection Act (in the Senate) and Corporate and Auditing Accountability and Responsibility Act (in the House). It is more commonly called Sarbanes–Oxley, Sarbox, or SOX. Whatever you call it, it is a federal law that attempted to set new standards of ethical behavior for management, board members, and employees of publicly traded companies. Some have claimed that the law increased compliance costs and caused IPOs to fall. This may not be the case, however. It is just as likely that a decline in ethics caused the fall in IPOs. Small and other businesses began to believe that you just could not trust Wall Street, and they either went to the private (as opposed to public) markets or did not obtain capital at all. This in part explains the elevated unemployment levels in the United States and elsewhere.

SEC is short for the U.S. Securities and Exchange Commission, the main regulatory agency charged with protecting the investing public.

Securities Act of 1933 is the law, modified by the JOBS Act, governing the sale of company ownership and loan interests or securities using the "means and instrumentalities of interstate commerce." All such offers and sales must be registered with the U.S. Securities and Exchange Commission. The law, which regulates original issue market activities, attempts to ensure that security buyers are fully informed before purchasing securities.

---

[2] For more, see www.investopedia.com/terms/i/ipo.asp#ixzz1wrZTVpwM.

Securities Act of 1934 governs what happens after you buy a security and wish to trade it. It establishes the rules for the secondary trading of securities. The 1934 Act also established the SEC.

Self-regulatory organizations are investment industry companies and individuals who come together to govern their business activities.

Summary

The JOBS Act is a significant change to the rules governing how companies raise money through the securities markets, which this book explains in detail. Among other things, it allows companies to raise more in "private placements" than in the past before having to register securities with the SEC, it allows companies to raise money through crowdfunding, and it loosens the rules regarding the advertisement of securities before they are sold.

Rules implementing this law have yet to be written, however, so there is a chance that innovators, entrepreneurs, and others may not be able to use the law as envisioned. Financial industry representatives, tied to the old way of doing things, may attempt to block or slow the use of the new capital raising freedoms granted by the act. But the hope behind the law is that the innovators and entrepreneurs—for whom I have written this book—will find it far easier to raise capital and thus create jobs and prosperity for many.

Startup Financing Environment

Why the JOBS Act Now?

Ask anyone who has tried to start a business over the last five years, or has been in business for a while, and he or she will tell you that this has been an extraordinarily tough environment. Yes, there are those for whom capital is not an issue, but these are the exceptions. Even long-existing companies have seen their lines of credit reduced, or eliminated overnight, by banks claiming that they were required to do so by regulators. When banks are told to reduce risk, small businesses, especially startups, are the first to see credit levels reduced—and lenders claim that this is an appropriate response to new regulatory guidelines.

We're not buying it. In response to being told to reduce risk, there is no reason to start by clamping down on small business credit. While banks are denying needed small business credit and not helping others issue IPOs, they are making risky bets with other people's money. Look no further than the $2 billion—or more—that J. P. Morgan lost in a recent hedging trade. They lost that money because people were trying to maximize profit, and bonuses, in a big way.

Now there's a way startups can avoid being at the mercy of bank policy, poor trades, and regulatory rulings. The JOBS Act offers a powerful set of tools startups can use to bypass banks: Crowdfunding.

■ **Note**　People have dreams. They have needs. They have talent and will create companies to make use of that talent and, in the process, fulfill those dreams. Crowdfunding is the result. The combination of an unresponsive financial sector, technology that allows anyone to eliminate the need for a middleman, and the optimistic and caring nature of the American people all serve to make this an exciting time.

Declining Startups

Not only has the credit environment been difficult, but attitudes toward business startups have suffered. Fewer people in the United States are inclined to take the very significant risks that are a part of starting a business. According to the latest data available from the Kauffman Foundation, in 2011, "the rate of business creation declined from 340 out of 100,000 adults in 2010 to 320 out of 100,000 adults in 2011, which represents a drop of 5.9%."[1] While this is a significant drop, Kauffman also notes that the rate at which adults started businesses in 2011 is still higher than it was in 2007, at the start of the recession. Don't be fooled. I believe the recession forced many individuals to start businesses—such as consulting, day care centers, and construction firms.

Impact of the Market Crisis on the IPO Market

Driven by greed, investment bankers often justify their outsized compensation by claiming they exist to serve the public by providing capital to new companies, that by bringing new companies to market they increase economic activity and provide for the social good. The Global financial market crisis of 2007–2012 provided experience and data many used to debunk that claim. Below, we provide additional information that can be used to test the investment banker's claim to "social good."

■ **Note**　Initial Public Offerings (IPOs) have been a primary way companies have raised significant amounts of equity capital. This money is ostensibly used to help the company grow (or to repay debt, thereby eliminating a burden and also setting the stage for corporate growth), and, unlike a loan, does not have to be repaid at fixed terms or with interest. Those

---

[1] From Robert W. Fairlie, The Kauffman Index of Entrepreneurial Activity, 1996 to 2011. Available at: www.kauffman.org/uploadedfiles/kiea_2012_report.pdf.

providing capital to the company, investors, depend on the stock market to set the subsequent price for the stock and, in turn, the value of the company selling the shares. The Bank of North America (chartered in 1781 and now Wells Fargo) launched the first IPO in the United States. As of July, 2012, the largest IPO ever was the $22 billion dollar Agricultural Bank of China offering in 2010. The $1 million annual JOBS Act fundraising limit represents 0.005% of this amount.

Over the last ten years, the number of companies raising capital through the issuance of stock in the public securities markets has declined dramatically. According to the IPO Task Force, a small group of professionals representing the investment industry and formed at the U.S. Treasury Department–sponsored "Access to Capital Conference" in 2011, "791 companies went public (issued stock) in 1996, and the U.S. averaged 530 IPOs per year from 1991 to 2000. By contrast, the U.S. averaged fewer than 157 IPOs per year from 2001 to 2008. In 2009, the U.S. had only 61 IPOs; in 2010, it had 153 IPOs." Figures 2-1 shows this information graphically.

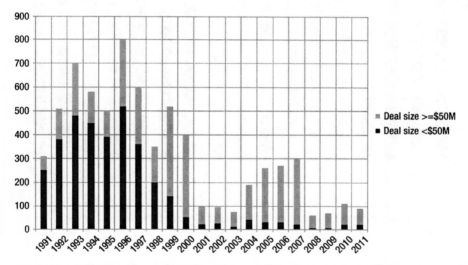

Figure 2-1. Decline in the number of IPOs. Source: IPO Task Force, a small group of professionals representing the investment industry and formed at the U.S. Treasury Department–sponsored "Access to Capital Conference," October 20, 2011.

In addition, the number of businesses created in the United States declined from March 1994 to March 2010. In 2007, 627,000 firms were started. Only 505,000 were started in 2010, a decline of 23% (see Figure 2-2).

▨ **Note** Some have claimed that these figures are misleading, and that companies simply turned to private market transactions to raise the needed equity. These are transactions between a company and private individuals, instead of between a company and the public. Others have claimed that regulatory issues have slowed the IPO market. These reasons, in our view, are likely to be false. The LIBOR (London inter-bank offered rate) scandal and the Facebook IPO show that more fundamental ethical factors may play the bigger role. What is unquestioned is that small companies are responsible for most of the new jobs created in the U.S. economy.

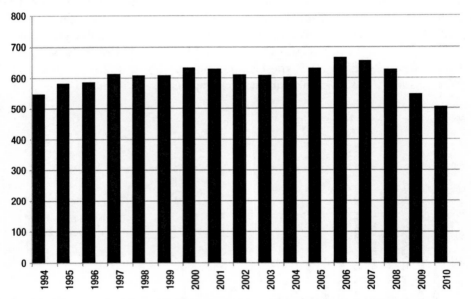

Figure 2-2. Number of Private sector establishments launched. Source: "Taking Action, Building Confidence: Interim Report of the President's Council on Jobs and Competitiveness," October 2011.

Investment banks turned away from the IPO market in favor of proprietary trading and other products that were easier to profit from. It's not that it was a bad time to do IPOs. According to the IPO Task Force, investors know that IPOs tend to perform well. It's just that they cannot get IPO shares fairly or regularly. In addition, there has been a lack of research and data on companies issuing IPOs.

In addition to denying deserving companies funding, this behavior damaged the competitive position of the United States. As U.S. investment banks turned away from this market, companies seeking IPO-generated capital took their business overseas. As the IPO Task Force noted, "U.S. companies raised only 15% of global IPO proceeds in 2010, down from an average 28% over the preceding ten years." This behavior is not only damaging to companies denied capital, it is damaging to workers. According to the IPO Task Force, "92% of job growth in a company occurs post-IPO."[2]

As the President's Council on Jobs and Competitiveness noted, had the U.S. "maintained the same level of startup activity that we witnessed in 2007, we would have nearly two million more jobs than we have today."[3]

Comparing the United States to China

One source, the Global Entrepreneurship Monitor (GEM), conducted its 13th annual survey of the environmental environment in 2011. The survey rates entrepreneurial activity around the globe.

GEM, an impressive and comprehensive survey tool, "interviewed over 140,000 adults (18–64 years of age) in 54 economies, spanning diverse geographies and a range of development levels. Based on this survey, GEM estimated that 388 million entrepreneurs were actively engaged in starting and running new businesses in 2011."[4]

Based on this source, Figure 2-3 compares early-stage entrepreneurial activity in China with that in the US. The chart shows that entrepreneurial activity is much higher in China than in the United States right now.

■ **Note**   China now leads the world in energy consumption, and energy consumption is a leading economic indicator. It is only a matter of time before China's economy surpasses that of the United States in size. Of course, this may change if enough US companies use crowdfunding.

---

[2] From Venture Impact 2007, 2008, 2009, and 2010 by IHS Global Insight; IPO Task Force August 2011 CEO Survey.

[3] Jobs Council, Report to the President: Taking Action, Building Confidence: Five Common Sense Initiatives to Create Jobs, October, 2011. Available at: www.jobs-council.com/recommendations/executive-summary-of-building-confidence-taking-action-interim-report/.

[4] From the Global Entrepreneurship Monitor 2011 Global Report.

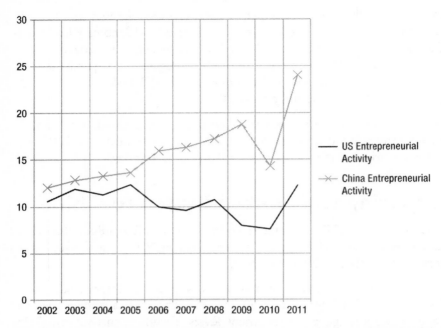

Figure 2-3. Total early-stage entrepreneurial activity, United States vs. China. Source: Global Entrepreneurship Monitor (GEM) 2011 Global Report. The vertical scale on the left is the percentage of the population, ages 18–64, who are either nascent entrepreneurs or owner-managers of new businesses.

Housing Crisis Thwarting Startups

Clearly, banking issues have significantly reduced the amount of capital available for new business financing. What's more, the housing crisis has reduced the amount of capital entrepreneurs can access. Why? Home equity loans finance many startups. As the Department of Commerce notes, "homes provide collateral and home equity loans provide relatively low-cost financing."[5]

Figure 2-4 shows the decline in the value of homes in the United States, 2002 to 2012.

---

[5] Robert W. Fairlie and Alicia M. Robb, "Disparities in Capital Access between Minority and Non-Minority-Owned Businesses: The Troubling Reality of Capital Limitations Faced by MBEs," U.S. Department of Commerce, Minority Business Development Agency, January 2010.

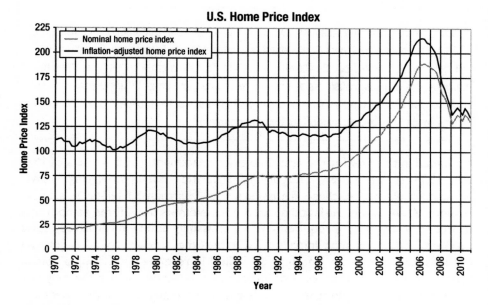

Figure 2-4. U.S. home price index. Source: JP's Real Estate Charts.[6]

Home equity provides a significant portion of a person's net worth, and, again, according to the Department of Commerce, "most studies find that asset levels (e.g., net worth) measured in one year increase the probability of starting a business by the following year. The finding has generally been interpreted as providing evidence that entrepreneurs face liquidity constraints."[7] Yet, despite the environment, a significant number of people want to own their own business. The pull to the path to financial freedom through successful entrepreneurship is strong, even with the financial crisis.

What the JOBS Act Does

Using new capital-raising techniques to start a business, the JOBS Act removes or eases at least one liquidity constraint or barrier.

It seeks to open domestic capital markets to small businesses and reform and to repair IPO market-access mechanisms.

---

[6] www.jparsons.net/housingbubble/US Median House Prices.xlsx

[7] Fairlie and Robb, p. 17.

▓ **Note**   Access and motivation are two critical parts of the entrepreneurship puzzle. The JOBS Act is unparalleled in its ability to address critical issues in this area. Entrepreneurs will self-identify, and the act, by allowing access to capital via crowdfunding, will help to motivate potential small business owners. As more and more small business projects are crowdfunded and become successful, we expect attitudes in the broader US society to change to show increased support for entrepreneurship.

Amended in this way for the first time since enactment, the SEC Acts of 1933 and 1934 create a new category of securities issuer, emerging growth companies. As noted, these are issuers with less than $1 billion in sales or revenue. As we saw in the last chapter, the act exempts these firms, temporarily, from certain regulatory requirements when issuing equity in regulated capital markets. While exempt initially, EGCs become subject to all regulatory burdens after five years. Reaching $1 billion in revenue and having a "public float"—market capitalization—of greater than $700 million are the only two other events that trigger the formerly exempted regulatory requirements.

The idea is that, after five years, reaching $1 billion in revenue, or having a market valuation of $700 million, an EGC will be larger, have more employees, and thus better able to handle reporting requirements. The law assumes (correctly) that these reporting requirements are expensive, in both money and time. Thus, the law establishes a "growth window" during which EGCs are exempt from certain regulatory requirements.

From Which Regulations Are EGCs Exempt?

EGCs get relief from only selected security market regulations. I presented the basic facts on some of these regulations in Chapter 1. What follows is an elaboration on the more important aspects.

Audited statements. The JOBS Act mandates that EGCs must provide audited financial statements for two, not three, years prior to stock issuance. One year after it issues stock, an EGC would be required to provide three years of financial data, if these exist.

Financial reporting. The JOBS Act exempts EGCs from accounting and financial reporting rules, mandated by the Public Company Accounting Oversight Board (PCAOB), requiring "mandatory audit firm rotation." This means that EGCs are not required to change auditors from one that knows the firm to one that does not.

Marketing. In order to help determine the probability that EGC offerings will be successful, the JOBS Act allows EGCs to canvass and communicate with qualified and institutional investors. Before the sale, EGCs must still provide a prospectus to potential investors.

Regulatory initiatives. EGCs are also exempt for certain provisions of more recent financial market regulatory initiatives. ECGs do not have to hold a "non-binding stockholder vote on executive compensation arrangements." They also do not need to calculate and report the "median compensation of all employees compared to that of the CEO."

Perhaps the most interesting thing is that the JOBS Act exempts EGCs from restrictions concerning the flow of information to investors from security analysts about these firms. Currently, investment banks and brokers cannot publish research on a specific EGC while offering that company's stock. Now, investors can receive EGC research reports "before or at the same time as its IPO."

Sarbanes-Oxley. Section 404(b) of Sarbanes-Oxley (P.L. 107-204) "requires a publicly-held company's auditor to attest to, and report on, management's assessment of its internal controls." Publicly traded firms must assess how effective inside controls over financial and accounting reports are in identifying and describing potential fraud. This internal evaluation must be review and certified by outside auditors. SOX 404 requires that publicly traded companies "establish and maintain internal controls over financial reporting." EGCs, under the JOBS Act, have up to five years to put into place these audit procedures.

The CEO and CFO of EGCs must still certify that the EGC's financial statements are accurate. Internal financial reporting controls are still required. These internal controls do not need to be reviewed and certified by outside auditors, however, for up to five years.

Section 501. In order to protect the investing public, Section 501 of SOX remains in place. Section 501 required the SEC to deal with and mitigate "potential conflicts of interest that may arise when research analysts recommend equity securities."[8]

To facilitate this activity, the JOBS Act allows EGCs to submit a preliminary confidential registration statement with the SEC. While the SEC can begin to evaluate EGC registration statements prior to IPO launch, an EGC must wait at least 21 days before soliciting potential investors en masse via road shows,

---

[8] David Hennes and Carmen J. Lawrence, "Memorandum: The Jumpstart Our Business Startups Act and Its Impact on Equity Research Analysts," Fried, Frank, Harris, Shriver & Jacobson LLP, May 18, 2012. Available at www.friedfrank.com.

defined as "a presentation by an issuer of securities to potential buyers intended to create interest in the securities."[9]

Summary

The JOBS Act is a much-needed shot in the arm for U.S. entrepreneurs. These individuals have been suffering greatly due to a banking system that ignored them in favor of easier profits; a regulatory system that let the banks do so; a housing crisis; and an increasingly competitive international climate.

Next, we get into the details of the JOBS Act.

---

[9] From Investopia. Available at: www.investopedia.com/terms/r/roadshow. asp#ixzz1wrWz8Wzn.

Disclosure and Crowdfunding in the JOBS Act

One of the major changes promulgated by the JOBS Act affects financial disclosures. Startups are relieved from many of the more burdensome accounting and reporting requirements, requirements imposed by the Securities and Exchange Acts of 1933 and 1934. This section describes these changes in detail, as well as the provisions relating to crowdfunding—using the Internet as a means to raise capital.

Chapter 4: Accounting, Reporting, and Other Standards in the JOBS Act: Relief from Regulatory Burdens

In Chapter 4 of this book, I describe changes the law makes to disclosure requirements. These are critical. Disclosure rules describe and govern the specific information that must be given to investors before and after they invest. These rules have been said to limit the ability of small firms to raise money. In an age in which information moves in the blink of an eye and people use the Internet to conduct business transactions of astonishing variety, it makes sense to use the technology to facilitate the flow of capital and other resources to create small business enterprises, especially when banks have not been lending.

Chapter 5: Crowdfunding

Chapter 5 describes crowdfunding, the key tool used to finance new small business startups. This is the ability of new and existing emerging growth companies (EGCs) to sell part of their company via equity shares over the Internet.

Chapter 6: Portals: Working with Your Partner

Chapter 6 discusses and describes portals, the intermediaries sitting between EGCs and investors. Portals are critical to the flow of capital to EGCs.

Emerging Growth Companies

Facts, Figures, and Potential

Of the 29,169,212 companies listed in the Manta[1] database, 25,346,594, or 86.9%, have less than $1 billion in reported revenue.[2] These are emerging growth companies in the United States. The JOBS Act targets these firms and allows them to raise up to $1 million in equity capital via crowdfunding on an annual basis. In this chapter, we examine the potential EGC market in general. At the end of the chapter, we show how EGC firms have used existing crowdfunding platforms to raise donations, but not equity. This will help us better understand how these platforms will help EGCs gain funding.

Table 3-1 shows the distribution of EGCs in the US by State.

---

[1] Manta has "the world's largest online community for promoting and connecting small business," and claims more than one million registered users and 87 million company profiles. From www.manta.com/coms2/page_faq.

[2] Available at: www.manta.com/mb?refine_company_rev=R01&refine_company_ rev=R02&refine_company_rev=R03&refine_company_rev=R04&refine_company_ rev=R05&refine_company_rev=R06&refine_company_rev=R07&refine_company_ rev=R08&refine_company_rev=R09&refine_company_rev=R10.

Table 3-1. Number of EGCs, by State or Territory (Source: Manta.com)

State or Territory	Number	State or Territory	Number
Alabama	365,898	Nebraska	168,624
Alaska	63,626	Nevada	200,140
Arizona	456,896	New Hampshire	125,507
Arkansas	227,357	New Jersey	725,730
California	2,957,306	New Mexico	146,830
Colorado	507,653	New York	1,493,161
Connecticut	327,058	North Carolina	750,962
Delaware	76,402	North Dakota	73,609
District of Columbia	83,384	Ohio	855,444
Florida	1,954,886	Oklahoma	289,232
Georgia	853,261	Oregon	347,395
Hawaii	94,445	Pennsylvania	944,279
Idaho	141,718	Puerto Rico	32,655
Illinois	947,463	Rhode Island	81,967
Indiana	464,615	South Carolina	344,085
Iowa	279,673	South Dakota	81,258
Kansas	237,052	Tennessee	496,710
Kentucky	324,872	Texas	2,077,742
Louisiana	392,740	Utah	218,302
Maine	118,943	Vermont	62,470
Maryland	480,929	Virgin Islands	1,690
Massachusetts	542,915	Virginia	620,455
Michigan	803,784	Washington	586,470
Minnesota	475,039	West Virginia	113,689
Mississippi	227,667	Wisconsin	465,308
Missouri	476,506	Wyoming	55,116
Montana	105,610		
United States		TOTAL	25,346,528

California, New York, Florida, and Texas have the largest number of firms with less than $1 billion in revenue. Wyoming has the fewest. While the geographic distribution is both important and interesting, note that these companies are everywhere. Also note that the number of firms may not be as important as the general rate of entrepreneurial activity in a region. According to the Kauffman Index of Entrepreneurial Activity, Arizona, Texas, California, Colorado, and Alaska have the highest rate of entrepreneurial activity. Activity increased most in Nevada, Georgia, Massachusetts, Tennessee, California, and Florida.

■ **Note** States will have an opportunity to develop specialized rules for EGCs seeking to raise capital via crowdfunding. I expect to see competition between states to encourage EGCs to stay or locate in their area. If you are thinking of raising capital as an EGC, be sure to see what incentives your state is offering.

The total EGC market potential is large—very large. If each EGC issued $1 million in equity, the resulting market would total $25 trillion dollars in capital. But we don't have to dream this large. Even $1 trillion in equity offerings would forever alter the size, scale, scope, and nature of the small business market in the United States. Of course, many of these firms have no interest in raising $1 million in capital, and many are far too small for an offering of this size to make sense. But the numbers give you some idea of how many firms fit with the definition established by Congress, so this is the total market potential.

In a later section of this chapter, we take a look at firms reporting less than $50 million in revenue, probably a better indication of true future crowdfunding market activity. For now we will continue to follow the Congressional definition of the EGC marketplace.

Table 3-2 shows the number of EGCs by industry. The business services, construction, healthcare, and retail industries have the largest number of EGCs.

Table 3-2. Number of EGCs, by Industry (Source: Manta.com)

Industry	Number	Industry	Number
Advertising & Marketing	124,773	Housing	23,589
Aerospace	4,978	Information Technology	83,191
Agriculture	1,062,915	Insurance	420,999

Industry	Number	Industry	Number
Apparel	61,734	Legal	781,536
Associations/Non-Profits	605,293	Machinery & Equipment	214,054
Automotive Services	807,143	Manufacturing	43,484
Beverages	24,525	Materials & Chemicals	143,474
Building & Construction	2,213,925	Media	118,692
Computer Hardware	58,900	Medical Equipment & Device	55,084
Computer Software	85,873	Nonclassifiable establishments	1,657
Consumer Electronics & Appliances	216,076	Other Business Services	3,926,950
Consumer Services	1,774,052	Other Consumer Products & Services	607,992
Defense	1,933	Other Public Sector	22,537
E-Commerce & IT Outsourcing	76,185	Other industry Products & Services	7,620
Educational Services	110,351	Passenger Car Leasing	614,407
Electrical	226,404	Pharmaceuticals	20,631
Electronics	11,502	Printing & Publishing	338,191
Energy & Resources	159,849	Professional Services	1,352,761
Environmental Markets	37,977	Real Estate	1,066,951
Fabrication	148,998	Restaurants & Bars	804,618
Financial	699,588	Shopping & Stores	2,373,029
Food	100,714	Telecommunications & Wireless	211,904
Food Processing	4,019	Textiles	11,808
Furnishings	130,480	Transportation & Shipping	104,757
Government	18,831	Travel & Leisure	757,405
Healthcare	2,389,929	Warehousing & Storage	82,215
All Industries		TOTAL	25,346,483

Figure 3-1 combines 2012 data from Manta with 2011 data from the Kauffman Foundation showing the level of entrepreneurial activity by state. The chart maps the number EGC firms in a given state with an indicator showing the level of entrepreneurial activity in that state. The chart shows that, in general, having a large number of EGCs in a state is positively related to entrepreneurial

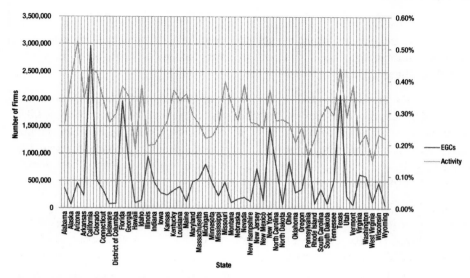

Figure 3-1. Number of EGCs and business activity.

activity in that state. This may be due to an increase in opportunities for entrepreneurial activity: the larger the set of firms, the more choice entrepreneurs have in terms of the entrepreneurial activity they may choose.

Note EGCs are everywhere. The data in Tables 3-1 and 3-2 show what type of competition you may face in your industry and your region. Understand, however, that this is no barrier to your raising funds. Your success depends upon your efforts, your network, your story.

Expect activity to increase, after some time, in highly entrepreneurial industries, like the construction industry, due to crowdfunding. It is conceivable that social service businesses, like child and senior care centers, will also see an increase in the number of firms in these industries. According to the Kauffman Index of Entrepreneurial Activity, the construction and the services sectors have the highest rates of entrepreneurial activity.

Note "The Kauffman Index of Entrepreneurial Activity is a leading indicator of new business creation in the United States. Capturing new business owners in their first month of significant business activity, this measure provides the earliest documentation of new business development across the country." From The Kauffman Index of Entrepreneurial Activity 1996-2011. Online at: www.kauffman.org/uploadedfiles/kiea_2012_report.pdf

If each of these firms used the nascent crowdfunding market to raise enough money to hire just one more person, that would result in 25 million new jobs, a huge number that shows the potential for this law to change the nature of small business activity in the country.

It is conceivable that the law will be most impactful in smaller industries and in smaller states. Why? Firms in these industries, like manufacturing (43,000 firms), and states, like Vermont (62,000 firms), typically have a more difficult time raising capital. The potential for growth and for developing new and more highly impactful business approaches will be higher in these "backwater" state and industries.

Also important are new, higher limits on money raised in more conventional ways. The JOBS Act allows firms to raise money using what are called Regulation A and Regulation D exemptions. Under the former, companies can now raise $50 million in capital, increased from $5 million. As to the latter, as one law firm noted, "Regulation D prohibited the general solicitation or advertisement of securities in Rule 506 offerings. Thus, issuers needed to have some preexisting relationship with potential purchasers before conducting a private placement. Title II of the JOBS Act has reversed that limitation to allow for the general solicitation and advertisement of a Rule 506 offering, as long as all ultimate purchasers are accredited investors."[3] These rule changes have the potential to allow companies to create a lot of jobs.

Of course, these two exemptions differ from crowdfunding. They are changes to existing exemptions and do not create a new class of small business firms and funding intermediaries. Even with these more generous provisions, the real fun and action is likely to be with EGCs on crowdfunding websites.

Crowdfunding Examples

Of course, what is exciting about the JOBS Act is the potential it has to significantly increase the number of small businesses operating in the United States. Crowdfunding sites like Kickstarter and Indiegogo have developed a record of assisting small ventures in their search for capital. To understand the businesses behind the numbers above, below I present a summary of several firms that have already sought to raise capital using crowdfunding. I will have more to say in Chapter 5 on crowdfunding sites, but in order to help

---

[3] Michael T. Rave, Ronald H. Janis, Frank E. Lawatsch, David A. Swerdloff, Lane T. Watson, Veronica M. Gonzalez, and Edward Bion Piepmeier. JOBS Act: On Regulation A, Regulation D and Crowdfunding Provisions. Day Pitney Alert. 4/19/2012. Available at: www.daypitney.com/news/newsDetail.aspx?pkID=4117.

you understand the truly revolutionary potential of this new financing mechanism, here we summarize the experiences of a few early adopters.

■ **Remember**   These are early adopters, some of the first and most successful crowd-funding examples. They are, by definition, exceptions. The key takeaway is this: Crowdfunding is the last step, not the first one, in raising capital online. You must bring the crowd with you.

Also note that these firms were not raising capital under the JOBS Act, since they are not issuing securities or selling equity stakes in their businesses. They are instead seeking donations, or selling a product. The existence of these sites, and their usefulness to young businesses, paved the way for the JOBS Act and its crowdfunding sections.

Pebble: E-Paper Watch for iPhone and Android

Perhaps the prototypical emerging growth company is Pebble Technology (Figure 3-2). The most successful crowdfunding initiative to date has been its Pebble Watch campaign. The watch connects wirelessly to a smartphone and serves as an on-the-wrist notification center.

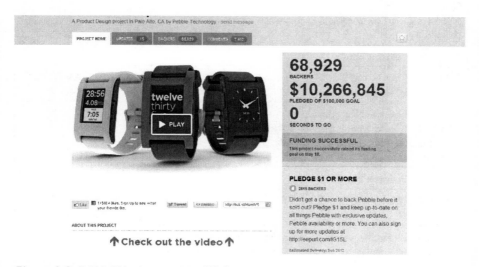

Figure 3-2. Pebble Watch campaign of Kickstarter.

Launched with a goal of raising $100,000, the campaign ultimately raised $10,266,845 from 68,929 backers or "investors." These individuals preordered one or more of the watches or paid $1 simply to be updated on the product's progress. Table 3-3 lists the "Perk" or sales list for the watch, showing what contributor got for participating in the fundraising.

Table 3-3. Pebble Watch Kickstarter Crowdfunding Donation "Perk" Listing[4]

PLEDGE $1 OR MORE	2615 BACKERS
Didn't get a chance to back Pebble before it sold out? Pledge $1 and keep up-to-date on all things Pebble with exclusive updates, Pebble availability or more. You can also sign up for more updates at http://eepurl.com/IG15L	
Estimated Delivery: Sep 2012	
PLEDGE $99 OR MORE	200 BACKERS SOLD OUT (0 of 200 remaining)
EARLY BIRDS Help us get started! One Jet Black Pebble watch. This watch will retail for more than $150. Free shipping to USA. (Add $10 for shipping to Canada, $15 for international shipping.)	
Estimated Delivery: Sep 2012	
PLEDGE $115 OR MORE	40799 BACKERS SOLD OUT (0 of 40799 remaining)
One Jet Black Pebble watch. Free shipping to USA. (Add $10 for shipping to Canada, $15 for international shipping.)	
Estimated Delivery: Sep 2012	
PLEDGE $125 OR MORE	14350 BACKERS SOLD OUT (0 of 14350 remaining)
One Pebble in any color (choose from Arctic White, Cherry Red, Voter's choice or Jet Black). Free shipping to USA. (Add $10 for shipping to Canada, $15 for international shipping.)	
Estimated Delivery: Sep 2012	
PLEDGE $220 OR MORE	3800 BACKERS SOLD OUT (0 of 3800 remaining)
Two Jet Black Pebble watches. Free shipping to USA. (Add $10 for shipping to Canada, $15 for international shipping.)	
Estimated Delivery: Sep 2012	

PLEDGE $235 OR MORE	100 BACKERS SOLD OUT (0 of 100 remaining)
HACKER SPECIAL You'll get early access to the SDK and we'll send you a prototype Pebble in August so you can get started coding. You will also receive another Pebble in any color when the full batch ships. Free shipping to USA. (Add $20 for shipping to Canada, $30 for international shipping.)	
Estimated Delivery: Aug 2012	
PLEDGE $240 OR MORE	4925 BACKERS SOLD OUT (0 of 4925 remaining)
Two Pebbles in any color (choose from Arctic White, Cherry Red, Voter's choice or Jet Black) Free shipping to USA. (Add $10 for shipping to Canada, $15 for international shipping.)	
Estimated Delivery: Sep 2012	
PLEDGE $550 OR MORE	900 BACKERS SOLD OUT (0 of 900 remaining)
OFFICE PACK Five Pebbles in any color (choose from Arctic White, Cherry Red, Voter's choice or Jet Black). Free shipping to USA. (Add $10 for shipping to Canada, $15 for international shipping.)	
Estimated Delivery: Sep 2012	
PLEDGE $1,000 OR MORE	482 BACKERS SOLD OUT (0 of 482 remaining)
DISTRIBUTOR PACK Ten Pebbles in any color (choose from Arctic White, Cherry Red, Voter's choice or Jet Black). Free shipping to USA. (Add $10 for shipping to Canada, $15 for international shipping.)	
Estimated Delivery: Sep 2012	
PLEDGE $1,250 OR MORE	20 BACKERS SOLD OUT (0 of 20 remaining)
CUSTOM WATCHFACE Let us create a custom watchface precisely to your specifications! Send us your ideas and we'll design a watchface just for you. You'll also receive 5 Color Pebble watches so you and your friends can share the fun. Free shipping to USA. (Add $10 for shipping to Canada, $15 for international shipping.)	
Estimated Delivery: Sep 2012	

[4] Source: "Pebble: E-Paper Watch for iPhone and Android, A Product Design project in Palo Alto, CA by Pebble Technology" campaign on Kickstarter. Available at: www.kickstarter.com/projects/597507018/pebble-e-paper-watch-for-iphone-and-android.

PLEDGE $10,000 OR MORE	31 BACKERS SOLD OUT (0 of 31 remaining)
MEGA DISTRIBUTOR PACK One Hundred Pebbles in any color (choose from Arctic White, Cherry Red, Voter's choice or Jet Black). Free shipping to USA. (Add $10 for shipping to Canada, $15 for international shipping.)	
Estimated Delivery: Sep 2012	

While encouraging, such success will not be typical. We expect most EGCs raising money over the Internet to more closely resemble the two firms described next.

East Harlem Café

On crowdfunding website Indiegogo.com Michelle Cruz, owner of the East Harlem Café, successfully raised $10,050 to purchase "kitchen storage, supplies and food prep equipment." Rather than going to a bank, Ms. Cruz turned to members of her community, via Indiegogo, to get the money she needed (Figure 3-3).

Figure 3-3. East Harlem Café campaign on Indiegogo.

Note that this was not, strictly speaking, an equity raise. Because the JOBS Act was not signed when this campaign was undertaken, it was, technically, illegal to raise equity financing over the internet. Instead, East Harlem offered a range of goods and services to those supporting the store via a cash donation. These are described in Table 3-4 and ranged from a "huge thank you" for a $1 dollar donation to a large coffee for a $10 donation, to an "all of the above" gift basket that included everything East Harlem offered to funders, plus exclusive use of the Café's space for two hours.

Table 3-4: East Harlem Café - Indiegogo Crowdfunding Donation "Perk" Listing[5]

Perks for your contribution	Donation Amount
Thank you!	$ 1
A huge thank you!	
Catch the Aroma	$ 10
The above plus + 1 Large Coffee	
Fork-Over	$ 20
All of the above + 1 dessert of your choice	
Be our Guest	$ 50
All of the above + Lunch on us!	
Dish-Out	$ 100
All of the above + Special shout-out on our newsletter and blog	
Dish-Out II	$ 100
All of the above + Special shout-out on our newsletter and blog + NEW PERK receive a Super-Fly East Harlem T-Shirt!	
Heap-Upon	$ 250
All of the above awesomeness + Super fly East Harlem T-Shirt + 1 bag of Fair Trade Coffee!	
Lavish-Upon	$ 500
All of the above's deliciousness + 1 two hour cooking class	
Feast	$ 1,000
All of the above + Exclusive two hour space rental	

The campaign was ultimately successful, raising $10,050 from 147 "investors."

What is important about this example is that is shows how a local firm, providing a high level of service to a specific community, can engage people

[5] *Source:* "Brewing Coffee and Culture" East Harlem Café Campaign on Indiegogo. Online at: www.indiegogo.com/eastharlemcafe?c=activity.

quickly and efficiently to obtain the funds needed. It goes without saying that the alternative funding source was a bank loan or a credit card. This firm was able to raise funds in less time than it would have taken them to get a bank loan and to reach out to customers, thereby generating an increase in revenue.

We have reproduced the firm's Indiegogo funding request below in Figure 3-4.

Simple. Honest. Effective. This will be the way most successful crowdfunders approach the market.

Figure 3-4. Indiegogo Campaign for East Harlem Cafe. Online at www.indiegogo.com/ eastharlemcafe.

La Casa Azul Bookstore

La Casa Azul is an independent bookstore in East Harlem.

This firm sought $40,000 and raised $34,503 from 433 "funders." La Casa is an example of another community-based business that energized its customer base to help the firm financially. Figure 3-5 lists their donation compensation or "perk" list.

Figure 3-5. La Case Azul campaign on Indiegogo.

Both campaigns raised far less than the $1 million dollar annual crowdfunding equity maximum now allowed by the JOBS Act. They also raised money in exchange for goods and/or services, not equity. Yet, these early campaigns are instructive in that they show how community businesses can raise significant amounts of money online, bypassing banks and other financial institutions and speaking directly with customers, in an engaging and truly remarkable way.

Summary

Emerging growth companies, as defined by the JOBS Act, are, like the country itself, a wildly varied lot. EGCs encompass everything from biotechnology firms with $100 million in venture capital funding to the hair salon next door. Every industry, every region, every city, every block hosts a potential EGC.

But there is strength in the diversity of firm sizes and types. Investors have a better chance of finding a firm or an industry that appeals to them. Some investors will seek to focus on a given industry or region. Some will focus on neighborhood businesses, say in East Harlem, New York. Some will focus on high-technology firms on the West Coast. Some may focus on auto parts stores in southwestern Iowa. The ability to focus small company investments will be astounding. Others will cast their crowdfunding investment net widely, subject to the limits imposed by the law. For these investors, diversification may limit the risk of loss for investors who are truly diversified. This is the true power of this effort.

Accounting, Reporting, and Other Standards in the JOBS Act

Relief from Regulatory Burdens

The Securities Act of 1933 mandates that to sell or even offer to sell securities in the United States, those securities must be registered with the Securities and Exchange Commission, the SEC. The SEC, in turn, requires security sellers (broker/dealers) to disclose a great deal of information about the company doing the selling, the company investors are buying into (not the funding portal or broker). This set of information tries to provide, comprehensively, all relevant information about the firm's past and future prospects. The Act of 1933 allows certain companies to skip the registration process under a limited number of conditions. These security registration exemptions generally allow a firm to sell its securities if it is selling them to "accredited investors," generally high-income, high net worth people.

▨ **Note** "Securities Act of 1933: Often referred to as the "truth in securities" law, the Securities Act of 1933 has two basic objectives: 1) require that investors receive financial and other significant information concerning securities being offered for public sale; and 2) prohibit deceit, misrepresentations, and other fraud in the sale of securities." Source: SEC. gov. Available at: www.sec.gov/about/laws.shtml.

But with the passage of the JOBS Act, requirements that small companies, or EGCs, abide by certain accounting and disclosure standards changed significantly.

In essence, the JOBS Act expands and modifies the number of financial security offering and sales exceptions. Exemptions are significant because they potentially lower the cost of raising capital. As you read, however, keep in mind that the exemptions outlined in the JOBS Act expire when one of three things happens:

1. The EGC reaches its fifth birthday after its IPO;

2. The EGC reaches $1 billion in revenue; and/or, finally,

3. The EGC becomes a "large accelerated filer."

A large accelerated filer is an issuer or firm with $700 million or more, as measured by its stock market value, in total equity shares in the hands of people who are not associated with the firm. The SEC measures these data as of the last business day of the second quarter of an issuer's fiscal year. A large accelerated filer is also a firm that has met certain SEC requirements, known as Section 13(a) or 15(d) requirements, for at least a year and has issued at least one annual report under these requirements.

Sections 13(a) and 15(d) mandate that companies offering securities submit certain periodic reports to the SEC. Figure 4-1 shows the recent 13(a) and d15(d) certification for Google, signed by Larry Page.

Finally, a large accelerated filer is one that is not entitled to use the exemptions that exist for smaller companies under other sections of the SEC Acts of 1933 and 1934.

Reporting Requirements the Act Relaxes

The JOBS Act seeks a gradual application of the more burdensome reporting requirements that publicly traded companies must bear to smaller companies.

In other words, as EGCs "grow up," they have to start playing by the same rules as the big boys. EGCs are still required to provide quarterly and annual reports. But, among other things:

- EGCs are exempt from Sarbanes-Oxley Section 404(b), meaning they are not required—for up to five years—to attest to internal audit controls.

- EGCs can provide two years' worth of audited financial statements prior to issuing stock, in place of the three years of statements, required before the passage of the JOBS Act. The exemption vanishes one year after the EGC offers stock, however, so that at year one, an EGC will need to report three years of audited financial data: the two years worth of data filed at the start of the period plus one year's worth of financial data collected in the interim.

- The act states that EGCs need not comply with new or revised financial accounting standards until those standards become "broadly applicable to private companies." EGCs can opt in, however, and choose to meet the requirements for certain regulations if they choose to do so before losing EGC status.

- EGCs do not need to change accounting auditors on the basis outlined in Sarbanes-Oxley. The auditors inspect accounting policies, practices, and procedures to make sure that they conform to standard industry practices and accurately reflect the financial condition of the firm. Under SOX, companies have to change auditors frequently to ensure no cozy relationships develop but EGCs do not, at least until their fifth birthday.

- EGCs do not need to calculate and display the ratio of "the median . . . annual total compensation of all employees (excluding the chief executive officer) to the annual total compensation of the chief executive officer" as required by Section 953(b)(1) of the Dodd-Frank Act.

Advertising and General Solicitation

Perhaps the most important change has been to the rules governing advertising and general security (stock or debt instrument) purchase or sale requests. Given the open nature of the Internet, if you are selling equity on the Web, it is very difficult, if not impossible, to restrict general advertising. The whole point of the Web is to allow access to information by people across the globe.

Note Rules governing hedge funds, private equity funds, and venture capital funds have been profoundly modified by the JOBS Act. Funds that rely on a Regulation D Rule 506 exemption will now be advertised and possibly be sold online. See my comments to the SEC on this: http://sec.gov/comments/s7-07-12/s70712-1.htm.

As part of the effort to encourage small companies to issue stock, Title II relaxes rules that limited the ability of firms to publicize or otherwise discuss their equity offering.

Rules limiting the ability of firms to ask people to buy or sell their stocks and bonds are well entrenched. In the United States, to be legal, offers to sell securities must meet certain requirements mandated by the SEC. Certain exemptions, called Regulation D exemptions, exist. But to be fully legal, a seller must abide by rules set by the SEC to have these exemptions apply to its sale of securities. The reason the JOBS Act is so important is that it creates a new set of security sales exemptions.

The JOBS Act tells the SEC to eliminate, or remove, any rules preventing security-instrument issuers from advertising to or otherwise soliciting persons from purchasing stock issued by small firms. This is known as "general solicitation" or "general advertising." Strangely, there is no formal definition in law for the terms "general solicitation" or "general advertising." Much like pornography cases at the Supreme Court, however, the SEC knows them when it sees them. The JOBS Act now allows potential investors to receive research from investment banks and others underwriting an EGC's IPO. Now, for example, an investment bank can provide research to potential investors in an EGC while serving as an underwriter to that EGC online and via other media. This makes sense only if you are going to offer equity online via a publically accessible website, since the investment bank and analyst have no way to control who accesses the information. Part of the problem with using the Internet to raise capital has been concern about possibly violating general solicitation and advertising rules. The changes that are part of the JOBS Act should eliminate these concerns.

Note General solicitation and general advertising are considered by the SEC as any advertisement, article, notice, or other communication published in any newspaper, magazine, or similar media or broadcast over television and radio, and any seminar or meeting whose attendees have been invited by any general solicitation or general advertising.[1]

---

[1] From: http://www.tollefsenlaw.com/answers/The-Law/Securities/General-Solicitation.asp

This is a major change. Previously, broker/dealers and investment banks could not provide research to most investors concerning the securities of small firms they were bringing to market.

SOX Conflict of Interest Provisions Still in Force

Conflict of interest provisions, as outlined in Section 501 of Sarbanes-Oxley, remain in effect. (Section 501 is included in the appendix.) In summary, these provisions require investment firms and analysts to keep research reports confidential prior to the time that the stock is offered to the public and to keep research reports free from influence by those seeking to sell investment banking services to issuers.

Section 501 requires investment analysts be supervised and evaluated only by investment firm personnel who are not involved in investment banking activities. The section also seeks to prohibit retaliatory actions targeting investment analysts who publish unfavorable reports on a company. Section 501 seeks to prevent this type of retaliation on the part of investment banking firm personnel who might feel that their firm's ability to solicit business from firms receiving unfavorable evaluations are diminished.

Under 501, investment banks that have or are about to participate in a security offering must establish certain time periods during which they halt the publication of research reports that provide information on certain issuers. Other actual and potential conflicts of interest, such as the analyst's personal investments in the company, or broker or investment banking firm compensation from the firm that is the subject of the report, must be disclosed. Likewise, status as an investment banking client in the one-year period before the report's publication, and any other material conflicts must be disclosed.

Accredited Investors

Under Title II of the JOBS Act, investment instrument sellers are required to verify that all equity security purchasers are accredited investors. (Note that these requirements do not apply to raising money through crowdfunding: Title III's provisions on spending and income limits serve the same purpose there.)

▓ **Note** Accredited investors are considered financially savvy and therefore better able to protect themselves from fraud.

Who or what is an accredited investor? Here's how the SEC defines it:

- A bank, insurance company, registered investment company, business development company, or small business investment company;

- An employee benefit plan, within the meaning of the Employee Retirement Income Security Act, if a bank, insurance company, or registered investment adviser makes the investment decisions, or if the plan has total assets in excess of $5 million;

- A charitable organization, corporation, or partnership with assets exceeding $5 million;

- A director, executive officer, or general partner of the company selling the securities;

- A business in which all the equity owners are accredited investors;

- A natural person who has individual net worth, or joint net worth with the person's spouse, that exceeds $1 million at the time of the purchase, excluding the value of the primary residence of such person;

- A natural person with income exceeding $200,000 in each of the two most recent years or joint income with a spouse exceeding $300,000 for those years and a reasonable expectation of the same income level in the current year; or

- A trust with assets in excess of $5 million, not formed to acquire the securities offered, whose purchases a sophisticated person makes.

To aid in determining the likelihood that a firm seeking to raise capital under the JOBS Act will actually be able to do so, the Act permits an EGC to communicate with potential institutional and qualified security buyers.

Crowdfunding: What EGCs Must Report

Table 4-1 shows what EGCs must provide to portals, and, by extension, to investors:

Table 4-1. EGC Reporting Requirements

- The EGC's name
- The ECG's legal status (corporation? partnership? LLC?)
- Actual physical address
- Virtual (website) address
- Names of all directors and officers
- Names of anyone owning more than twenty percent (20%) of the shares of the EGC
- EGC business description
- ECG anticipated business
- EGC financial condition, including:
  - EGC income tax return (if any) and CEO-certified financial statements for an EGC raising $100,000 or less
  - CPA-validated financial statements if the EGC is raising between $100,000 and $500,000
  - Audited financial statements for EGCs raising more than $500,000
- Proposed use of funds raised
- Targeted amount raised, with progress reports
- Price of the EGC securities and the way in which that price was determined
- Final EGC security price
- All required disclosures
- Opportunity to "rescind the commitment to purchase the securities"
- EGC ownership and capital structure
- EGC security terms for all securities of the issuer
- EGC security term modification procedures. (Details how the terms and conditions of the equity security offered can be changed.)
- Summary of the differences between all EGC securities
- EGC securities rights, including information on any material dilution, or qualification
- Impact of rights held by the principal shareholders of the EGC might impact the purchasers
- Name and ownership level of each existing shareholder who owns more than 20% of any class of the securities of the issuer
- Valuation methods, with example
- All risks to EGC security buyers

Keep in mind that, while this looks like a lot of data (and it is), most startups will not have to worry about providing much of it. I believe that most new crowdfunded startup firms will have one owner. This owner will hold, prior to the offering, 100% of the firm. This means the firm's capital structure will be as simple as possible: one owner holding all of the stock. The firm won't have issued any other securities, so no information needs to be provided about them since they don't exist. Documentation and terms concerning ownership rights will be standardized and made as fair and simple as possible to facilitate the offering. Valuation and security pricing will also be simple: the stock price is what it is; take it or leave it. You will, however, have to explain how you came up with that number.

> *Most startups will not have to worry about reporting the more difficult parts of the required data.*

Crowdfunding portals will help small business owners comply with these requirements. They will provide valuation models or modeling services, legal documents that describe the security rights, modification, and dilution information. For a one-person firm, these will be as simplified as possible, anyway.

In point of fact, we believe that portals with overly complicated terms and offerings will be seen as inauthentic and nontransparent. Crowdfunding investors will probably avoid these portals in favor of those that can comply with these requirements, while keeping things as simple as possible.

Note The best portals will simplify the crowdfunding process while maintaining the investor protection intent of the disclosure rules embedded in the JOBS Act.

Registration documents, including a prospectus, must be delivered to potential buyers prior to the sale of securities. These statements have, in the main, two parts. The prospectus describes key facts about the issuer's operation, how it is doing financially, and who runs the firm. A second portion of the registration document contains information that, while public, is not required. This can include anything from the firm's annual report, to contracts, to legal documents.

Table 4-2 provides more information on reporting requirements for EGCs and funding portals.

Table 4-2. Reporting Requirements for EGCs

JOBS Act EGC Reporting Requirements	Responsibility	Explanation
The name, legal status, physical address, and website address	EGC	Most EGCs will provide basic information, as required.
The names of the directors and officers (and any persons occupying a similar status or performing a similar function), and each person holding more than twenty percent (20%) of the shares	EGC	For most EGCs, this will be one or two persons.
A description of the EGC financial condition, including:		
$100,000 or less: Income tax returns for the most recently completed year (if any) and financial statements certified by the principal executive officer	EGC	Most EGCs will provide this information, as required.
More than $100,000, but not more than $500,000: Financial statements reviewed by an independent public accountant		Most EGCs will provide this information, as required.
More than $500,000: audited financial statements		Few EGCs will seek this level of funding. Those that do will have the financial resources to be able to comply with this requirement.
The target offering amount, deadline, and regular updates regarding progress	FP	Most of these reporting requirements will be facilitated by the funding portal.
The price to the public of the EGC securities or the method for determining the price. Final price and all required disclosures, with an opportunity to rescind.	FP	A Standardized Security Pricing Model (SSPM) will be developed by funding portals, along will all required legal certifications, including the rescission right.

JOBS Act EGC Reporting Requirements	Responsibility	Explanation
A description of the EGC ownership and capital structure, including:		
Terms of securities offered and each other class of security, including rules to modify and summary of the differences between securities, including how rights may be limited, diluted, qualified	FP	A Standardized Security Offering Document (SSOD), or prospectus, will be developed by funding portals, along with all required legal certifications, including the rescission right.
A description of how exercise rights held by the principal shareholders could negatively impact crowdfunding shareholders.	FP	An SSOD, or prospectus, will be developed by funding portals, along with all required legal certifications, including a description of how exercise rights held by the principal shareholders could negatively impact shareholders.
Name and ownership level of each existing shareholder with more than 20%	NM	These reporting requirements will be irrelevant for most firms, since they will be owned by one or two persons, In addition, the SSOD, or prospectus, will address this issue. Even in cases where there are many owners, this is a straightforward reporting requirement.
A description of the stated purpose and use of the proceeds. A description of the business of the issuer and the anticipated business plan:	EGC	Most EGCs will provide basic information, as required.

JOBS Act EGC Reporting Requirements	Responsibility	Explanation
How the securities being offered are being valued, and examples of future valuation methods, including the impact of subsequent corporate actions	FP	An SSPM will be developed by funding portals, along with all required legal certifications, including examples of future valuation methods, and the impact of subsequent corporate actions.
Risks relating to minority ownership, corporate actions, additional issuances, sale, assets sale, or transactions with related parties	FP	An SSOD, or prospectus, will be developed by funding portals, along with all required legal certifications, including risks relating to minority ownership, corporate actions, additional issuances, sale, assets sale, or transactions with related parties.

EGC = emerging growth company; FP = funding portal; NM = not meaningful.

Registration with the SEC

The JOBS Act permits EGCs to file a confidential registration statement with the SEC before launching their IPO. This allows EGCs to determine market demand for their securities without letting others know they are doing so and without exposing potentially sensitive business information. In addition, EGCs are allowed to meet with institutional and other accredited investors to determine the level of market interest in their securities.

▓ **Note**   Being able to gauge investor interest before offering stock is critical. The best portals will develop tools to accurately measure and facilitate this.

EGCs are required, in fact, to file, with the SEC, an initial confidential registration statement "at least 21 days before it begins pre-IPO road shows for potential investors."

Finally, EGCs are exempt from the requirements of section 229.301of Title 17, Code of Federal Regulations for any period prior to the earliest audited period presented in connection with its initial public offering. This regulation requires an issuer to provide the following data (the full set of requirements is included in the appendix):

- Net sales or operating revenues

- Income or loss from current operations

- Income per share

- Total assets

- Long-term debt

- Preferred stock

- Cash dividends per share

- Other financial data metrics that "would enhance an understanding" of the issuer's financial conditions and trends in operations

Under the old rule, these data had to be provided for the last five fiscal years or, if the issuer had been around for less than five years, for the life of the issuer and its predecessors. Issuers must, however, provide information for preceding fiscal years that is needed to keep the submitted data from being misleading.

Summary

The JOBS Act makes significant modifications to the rules concerning what companies must disclose to investors. In addition, it allows firms to "test the waters" more vigorously, communicating with a wider range of potential investors without having to publicly reveal sensitive, confidential business information.

Given the medium used to effectuate crowdfunding transactions, the Internet, the JOBS Act establishes that persons and companies with websites matching EGC stock buyers and EGC issuers will not have to register as a broker/dealer, unless they fail to meet certain conditions. It establishes that communications between EGCs and potential investors can happen under a wider range of circumstances, and establishes that even persons and institutions who may be involved in a crowdfunding transaction can distribute EGC research reports on a more reasonable basis. This facilitates the flow of information about EGCs and should lower the cost of raising capital.

5

Crowdfunding

Perhaps the most exciting part of the JOBS Act relates to crowdfunding. This chapter describes crowdfunding in detail and reviews how small businesses can use the technique to raise money.

What Is Crowdfunding?

Crowdfunding is a business financing technique that uses online social networks linked to a Web-based platform to raise money. It is as if, by having a Facebook page, you can generate donations (business financing capital) to finance something like an artistic project, a product, or a company. Imagine being able to raise money for your firm via eBay. Figure 5-1 illustrates a typical crowdfunding path.

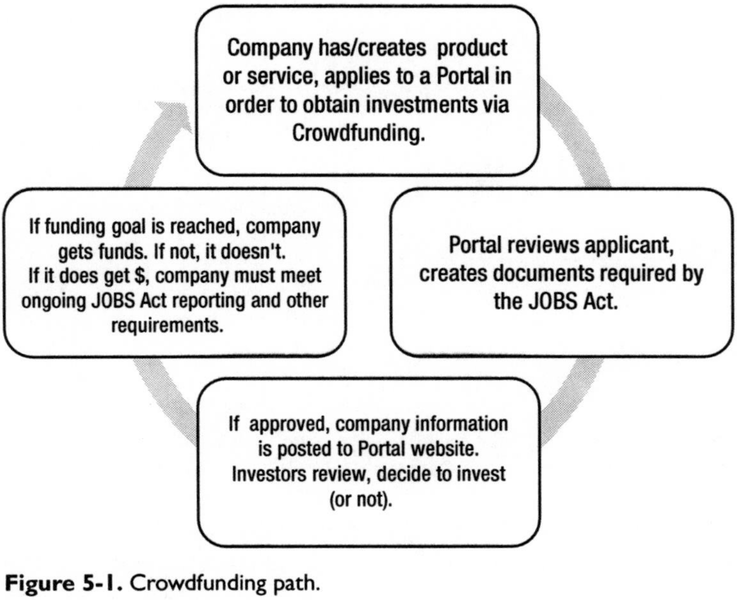

Company has/creates product or service, applies to a Portal in order to obtain investments via Crowdfunding.

If funding goal is reached, company gets funds. If not, it doesn't. If it does get $, company must meet ongoing JOBS Act reporting and other requirements.

Portal reviews applicant, creates documents required by the JOBS Act.

If approved, company information is posted to Portal website. Investors review, decide to invest (or not).

Figure 5-1. Crowdfunding path.

Using social networks to generate financing is nothing new. The Obama campaign used crowdfunding to raise $500 million in 2008.[1] The crowdfunding provision of the JOBS Act simply applies this experience to the practice of business financing. What is now different is that the JOBS Act validates and extends this approach to the business world. This is a huge change. In fact, it's the biggest change in business financing options since the creation of the small business loan. It has the potential to become what's called a *disruptive innovation*—a game changer in the world of finance.

Prior to the JOBS Act, people had been able to raise donations for a project or take orders (and money) for a product or service before launch. But until now, they have not been able to sell an interest in their firm legally.

Figure 5-2 gives a view of the potentially disruptive nature of crowdfunding.[2]

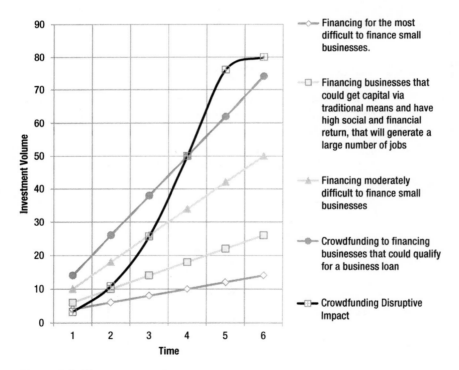

Figure 5-2. The potentially disruptive impact of crowdfunding.3

[1] Jose Antonio Vargas, "Obama Raised Half a Billion Online," *The Washington Post*, November 20, 2008. Available at: http://voices.washingtonpost.com/44/2008/11/20/obama_raised_half_a_billion_on.html.

[2] A description is available at: http://en.wikipedia.org/wiki/Disruptive_innovation.

[3] Adapted from Joseph L. Bower and Clayton M. Christensen, "Disruptive Technologies: Catching the Wave," *Harvard Business Review*, January–February 1995.

The bottom axis looks at the flow of business capital over time. The vertical axis is a scalar representing an index of the amount of money flowing to all firms. The line at bottom represents the amount of business startup funding directed to firms that would otherwise find it very difficult, if not impossible, to obtain financing. The next higher line represents firms that could get capital with some difficulty. Next are firms that can get capital from traditional institutions, and have very high social return, that is, they employ a large number of people and produce goods and services recognized as socially useful. Finally, the highest line represents firms for which obtaining capital is, with the proper documentation, not a problem. The curved black line shows the cumulative supply of capital to all of these firms, as augmented by crowdfunding.

■ **Note**   Other disruptive technologies include the graphical browser (vs. text based browsing), digital photography (vs. chemically based photography), GPS (vs. paper maps), telephones (vs. writing), USB drives (vs. floppy disks).

Currently, crowdfunders obtain donations or sell a product or service for cash. You have not been able to sell (legally) equity shares in your business online in the United States to nonaccredited investors. Until now.

Crowdfunding in the JOBS Act

Title III of the JOBS Act establishes the crowdfunding exemption, a release from legal liability that would otherwise arise from federal laws concerning the sale of equity securities under the Securities Act of 1933 (15 U.S.C. 77d). Trying to sell ownership stakes in very small companies via the Internet would be impossible otherwise. This is why the current crowdfunding models use donations or product preorders (as in the example of the Pebble Watch in Chapter 3.) to raise money. The securities laws are so burdensome that it is impossible to raise money (legally) any other way.

Once again, Title III says EGCs can sell up to $1 million in equity securities via crowdfunding over any 12-month period.

It also establishes that any individual can invest only the greater of $2,000 or 5% of either what they make or of their net worth (what they own minus what they owe) if their income or net worth is less than $100,000. Persons with a net worth or annual income greater than $100,000 can invest up to 10% of what they make in a given year in all EGC securities. The maximum persons with a net worth greater than $100,000 can invest is either 10% of their income or net worth, up to $100,000.

Income and Investment Limits

Figures 5-3 and 5-4 show income and investment limits. Figure 5-3 shows income on the left side and the investment limits on the right. It shows that, as income goes from $100,000 to $40,000, the limits drop from $10,000 to $4,000. From there, as income falls to $20,000, the crowdfunding investment limit declines to $2,000. Notice that $2,000 is the lower limit. In other words, even if you income is zero, you can still invest $2,000 in crowdfunding securities (assuming you can get $2,000 from somewhere.)

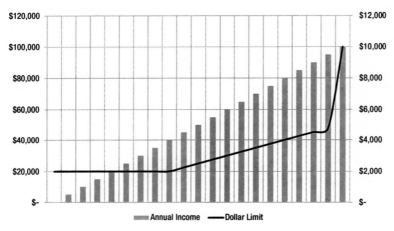

Figure 5-3. Crowdfunding investing limits for persons with incomes from $0 to $120,000.

Figure 5-4 shows income on the left side and the investment limits on the right. It shows that, as income drops from $6,500,000 to $100,000, the crowdfunding investment limit drop from $500,000 to $10,000.

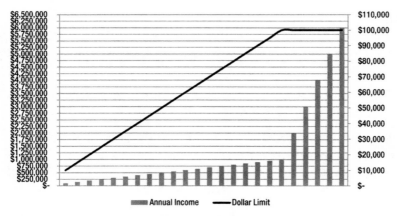

Figure 5-4. Crowdfunding investing limits for persons with incomes from $250,000 to $6,500,000.

Transactions must be conducted through a broker or funding portal that meets the requirements set out in Section 4A(a) of the JOBS Act. Issuers must comply with requirements set out in Section 4A(b) of the act. (I detail both sections in Chapter 9, which covers Title III of the act.)

Rules for Portals

To qualify to sell ECG securities, a broker or funding portal must register with the SEC as a broker/dealer or funding portal, must register with FINRA or another self-regulatory organization, must provide investors with both education and disclosures concerning the risk of monetary loss, and must ensure that investors actually read and understand educational and risk-of-loss documentation. Some question how anyone can verify another person's level of comprehension, but the JOBS Act mandates that funding portals try to address this issue. (I'll discuss this further in Chapter 6 on portals.)

A portal or broker/dealer must quiz EGC investors to document their understanding of the riskiness of these securities. They must also take steps to reduce the risk of fraud by obtaining a background check, including securities enforcement regulatory history, for persons holding more than 20% of the outstanding equity of each EGC issuer.

Portals also have to make sure EGCs are not funded until they reach monetary goals set at the start of the capital raise. In other words, if you say you are trying to raise a million dollars through crowdfunding, a crowdfunding portal cannot actually give you any money until pledges to your firm or the amount of money you raise actually totals $1 million. These funds will be held in a separate account. Some portals will not be able to actually hold funds. Some will. Either way, if you do not raise the targeted amount, all funds revert to your potential investors.

All investor information is confidential. Portals cannot compensate anyone for providing information on potential investors. Directors, officers, and partners in a funding portal cannot have a financial interest in EGC issuers launched on their portal.

Rules for Issuers

Section III of the JOBS Act further mandates that EGC issuers provide a lot of information to potential investors. As detailed in Chapter 4, this information includes data on the firm's (or the owner's) name and legal status (corporation, partnership, etc.). You must also include information on your physical location, so you need an address. EGC issuers also must report and provide information on anyone holding more than 20% of the shares of the firm raising cash. The current or projected anticipated business has to be described in a business plan.

You must describe the firm's current financial condition. For offerings less than $100,000, the income tax returns of the issuers or financial statements certified by the CEO; offering between $100,000 and $500,000 require CPA-reviewed financial statements; offerings greater than $500,000 require audited financial statements.

In addition, you must tell what you plan to do with the money, how much money you are trying to raise and when.

EGC issuers must provide regular updates concerning progress in meeting this goal.

You must set a price in writing for the securities offered, along with information on how that price was determined, and how it might be determined in the future. You must provide valuation examples. Investors must be given a reasonable opportunity to change their minds about the purchase.

Next, outline the current structure of the firm: who owns what, how, and when. Describe the terms, spelling out the conditions of the security offering, and outline information on the conditions surrounding both the security sale and the company. Describe any other ownership interests in the EGC firm offering the securities in detail. In addition, you have to describe information on certain conditions and terms of the ownership interest, along with information on how the rights in these ownership interest held by the current company owner(s) might be modified to damage the new prospective owners buying shares via crowdfunding.

In short, you must outline all risks, including risks relating to the fact that those purchasing shares in an EGC over the Internet are probably not the majority owners. Risks relating to ownership dilution, the sale of additional shares that reduce the percentage ownership of legacy or prior shareholders in a firm, must be described.

The EGC cannot advertise terms of the offering, except through "notices which direct investors to the funding portal or broker" and, until the SEC issues rules, cannot compensate anyone to promote its offerings.

EGC issuers are strictly liable for any material misstatements and omissions. EGC security buyers can bring a legal action to recover the amount of money they paid for an EGC security against EGC security offerors if they determine that the offerors left something out, hid relevant facts about the EGC, or shaded facts in a way that made the EGC appear more favorable and worthy than it actually was. The act establishes that persons can bring a legal action to recover moneys lost or for damages even if they no longer own the EGC security at issue.

Figure 5-5 provides a summary of crowdfunding as outlined in the JOBS Act.

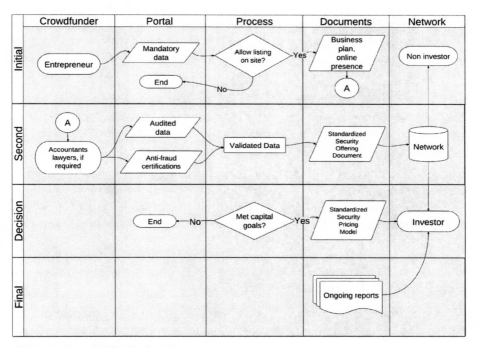

Figure 5-5. Crowdfunding process map.

The far left (first) column shows entrepreneurs as they approach the crowdfunding market. The next column represents portals, online crowdfunding facilitators. Critical portions of the crowdfunding process are shown in the middle column. Significant crowdfunding documents are in the next column, Finally, the column at right represents the crowdfunding network of investors and others. Notice that the first and last columns show people involved in the process. The rows represent phases of the process, defined as initial phase, the second phase, the decision phase, and the final phase.

Entrepreneurs start by providing mandatory data to portals, in the next column. The first decision point of the process is reached. Portals must decide if they will allow the entrepreneur to list his or her solicitation on the site. If so, the process continues, and business plans are posted. The process moves to connector A. Notice that at this point, there are no investors, hence the non-investor box in the last column.

Moving to connector A in the first column of the second row of the graphic, unaudited and audited data are collected by portals. Professional service providers, represented by accountants and lawyers, now join the process, depending upon the nature of the crowdfunding campaign. These service providers may or may not be required, depending upon the amount of money being raised. (The figure assumes these service providers are engaged.) They create audited financial reports and the anti-fraud certifications required by the Act. These validated data are used in the next phase of the process. A standardized security document is created and distributed to the network of potential investors.

At this point, note that the network is divided into two categories: noninvestors and investors. Investors receive information from a standardized security pricing model, as required by the Act. Non-investors do not.

Portals are required by the act to track fundraising goals for each company seeking funding. If the firm meets its fundraising goals, it moves to the final phase of the fundraising effort. Crowdfunding companies are required to provide regular updates to investors, represented in the graphic by the box labeled ongoing reports.

Nature of the Innovation

While not fully revolutionary, crowdfunding is a sustaining innovation, an evolutionary change that puts business financing within reach of everyone with an Internet connection, representing a true democratization of business capital access. Venture capital firms, commercial banks, and angel investors won't just stop lending and investing. They will continue to do so. They may now face new and significant competition, however.

Of course, crowdfunding is no panacea. The potential for fraud still exists. There is always the chance that someone will seek to create a fictitious funding portal or nonexistent company to raise money. Legitimate firms may fail, giving rise to a multitude of lawsuits that decimate interest in this new field, making it impossible for even worthy companies to raise capital. Or it may work too well. Thousands of small businesses may obtain capital without going to a bank or other financial institution. Banks and VC firms may then lobby to get the JOBS Act repealed.

In fact, there is every reason to believe that entrenched industry interests may mobilize to limit the reach and impact of this technology, since this tends to happen with every disruptive business innovation. Investment and commercial banks would try to limit the power of this financing technique, since it has the potential to reduce their control over the small-business lending market.

Advantages of Crowdfunding

Crowdfunding has a number of advantages. Using crowdfunding, small business owners can bypass the Small Business Administration, and leave other ineffective small business financiers behind.

Perhaps the biggest advantage of crowdfunding over traditional financing is that it enables entrepreneurs to gauge public interest in their product and service and obtain financing at very low cost. If successful, investors in the project often become "network evangelists," bringing others to the table to buy both products and shares in the new firm. Traditional venture capital firms have tried to do this by creating a network of investee firms that use goods and services created by other companies in which the VC has invested. Questions concerning the fairness and ethics of this "VC network" approach are well known, but this is not an issue with crowdfunding. That's because crowdfunding seeks to create an authentic, diversified, and diverse group of investors in an EGC, which places it beyond the control of any single VC firm.

▨ **Note** Venture Capital (VC) firms invest in startup and early-stage firms. Venture capital investments usually start at $250,000 and are mainly made to businesses with the possibility of very high growth If they invest, these firms expect to earn a significant return on their investment. For example, in 1996 one venture capital firm, invested $2 million dollars in Lycos, an Internet search engine. That investment was worth $427 million at the start of 1999.

In addition to creating or validating the market for your service/product, crowdfunding enables you to control the financing process in a way that no other business financing option allows. An entrepreneur controls all aspects of the offering, from the dollar amount sought, to the timing of the issue, to the amount paid for assistance. Some portals (those that are affiliated with SEC-registered broker-dealers) will be allowed to charge for their services, but if a given portal seems to charge too much, others will probably spring up to offer crowdfunding services at a discount. Small investors are likely to be patient investors, too, and more willing to wait until the product or service proves itself in the marketplace, since the law prohibits them from placing the bulk of their net worth in any one venture.

Crowdfunders are responsible for all aspects of the effort, from choosing the site on which to list to creating a "pitch" and other solicitation documents, to setting the terms of the transaction. Portals and broker dealers may structure the documents and give you options, but the final decision rests with the crowdfunded company. If they do not like listing conditions on one portal website, they will go to another with better terms. In addition, crowdfunders do not, of necessity, need to give up a significant or majority portion of their ownership in their company to get money. Of course, what is a reasonable share of the firm to give up will vary. Standards will develop over time.

Most crowdfunders set a financial goal, in terms of the amount of money they are seeking to raise, but may exceed it. In what must be the most watched crowdfunding campaign, the Pebble: E-Paper Watch for iPhone and Android (Pebble Watch) sought to raise $100,000 and managed to raise over $10,000,000.[4] (I discuss this effort above.)

In addition to the advantages noted above, note that, in most cases, if the initial effort to raise capital is unsuccessful, a business owner can retool their approach, typically using feedback obtained from his or her unsuccessful campaign, and try again. While the act puts an "all or nothing" rule in place, this has not traditionally been the case in the field. Some current sites allow crowdfunders to take what they have raised.

Drawbacks of Crowdfunding

As with any new instrument, there are drawbacks to this type of funding. It may not work. You may spend a great deal of time and effort trying to raise money, only to fall short. This can be stressful. Crowdfunding requires a level of transparency and openness that other forms of financing do not. To be successful, the crowdfunding effort must be consistent and diligent. This means that most successful crowdfunding efforts are well thought out, stay in constant contact with potential funders, and tell one story and stick with it. They may add data at the request of individuals, but they do not start by raising money for a film, for example, only to change to raising money for a book if they cannot raise enough to make a film.

The number of investors you will have to deal with via crowdfunding is typically far larger than that with traditional business financing. This, too, can be stressful. With traditional business financing, the number of investors an entrepreneur has to deal with (and keep happy) tends to be very small—one bank; one venture capital firm; or a few friend, family and/or angel investors.

In addition, despite the ethical issues noted above, for certain firms and in certain industries, the advice and counsel traditional investors provide can be invaluable. Taking advice from a thousand small investors may be, at best, impractical.

---

[4] Available at: www.kickstarter.com/projects/597507018/pebble-e-paper-watch-for-iphone-and-android.

▓ **Note** The crowdfunding market is also likely to become saturated with similar projects. How one distinguishes oneself, without giving away trade secrets, is bound to be a key question.

A Charitable Word

What if you just need a few dollars to pay a bill, handle a medical emergency, fund a short-term project or event? You don't really want to create a company through crowdfunding to do so. Can crowdfunding still help? Yes. Many sites exist to fund these types of needs and projects. One is GoFundMe. GoFundMe allows you to set up a personal online fundraising website. It serves as a useful alternative and counterpoint to the business financing approach, while providing data that can be useful for those seeking to crowdfund a business.

GoFundMe has been around for two years. In that time, it has grown to the point of now facilitating almost $2 million in charitable donations per month. Figure 5-6 outlines its growth.

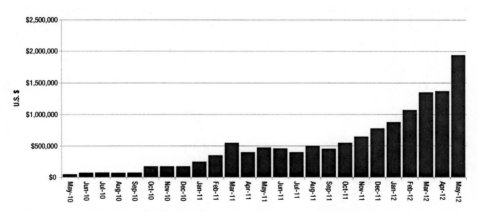

Figure 5-6. GoFundMe monthly payment volume, showing the amount of money raised each month, data up to May, 2012. Released June 29, 2012.

Figure 5-7 shows the types of projects funded on the GoFundMe website by category.

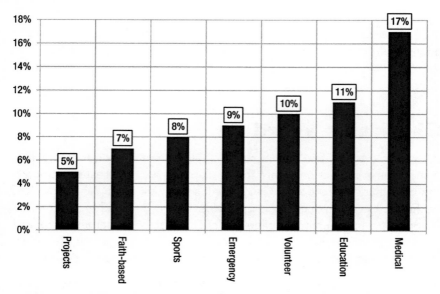

Figure 5-7. GoFundMe Projects, by type of solicitation, as of June 29, 2012.

By way of introduction to crowdfunding in general, Figure 5-8 shows the number of GoFundMe users who connect to Facebook (46%) and the number of GoFundMe projects that sought less than $1,000 (76%).

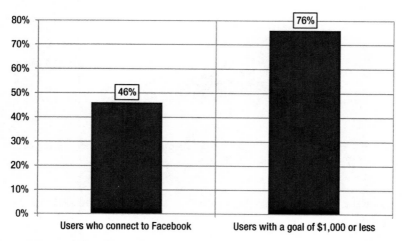

Figure 5-8. GoFundMe users—connection to Facebook and percentage of campaigns seeking less than $1,000.

Finally, Figure 5-9 shows that GoFundMe users had, on average, 482 Facebook friends and raised $1,126.00 on average.

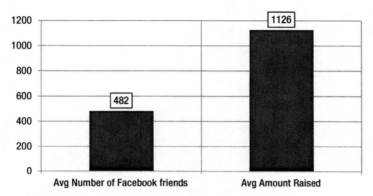

Figure 5-9. Average number of Facebook friends and average amount raised on GoFundMe, as of June 29, 2012.

Lessons:

1. If you just need money for a project or a personal issue, use a charitable donation focused crowdfunding website, like GoFundMe. Do not try to create a business to deal with a personal issue or project.

2. On the charitable donation side, successful projects solicit small dollar amounts. This lesson applies to business crowdfunding as well. The impact of fraud and misapplication of funds raised are minimal if the dollar amount sought is small.

3. You must bring people to the crowdfunding party. These will probably be Twitter, Facebook, LinkedIn and other social media friends, supplemented by non-social media friends. This lesson applies to donation- and business-based projects.

Figure 5-10 summarizes these relationships. The graphic includes three crowdfunding websites, each representing a different sector.

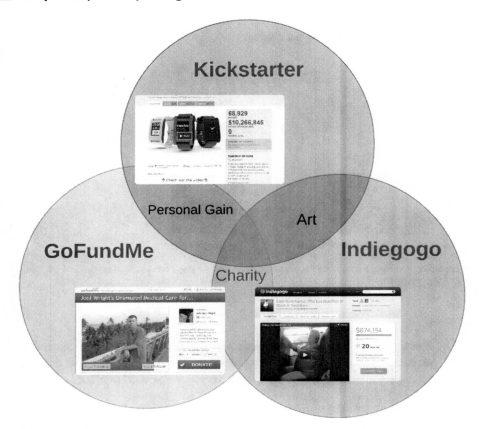

Figure 5-10. Relationship between current crowdfunding websites, by types of solicitations.

Kickstarter is closest to a website focusing on for-profit ventures, given its success with the Pebble Watch. Kickstarter also has an affinity for art and artistic projects, including computer software. Indiegogo also has a large number of artistic projects on its site. GoFundMe seems to focus on the charitable, with many projects that seek to provide financing for personal medical and other health-related needs. Where Kickstarter and GoFundMe seem to overlap is in the fact that these projects might be considered those that are focused on meeting personal needs or achieving personal gain. This does not mean all of these projects are selfish, just that they are personal. Indiegogo and GoFundMe seem to focus on artistic and personal projects. These are rough approximations of the focal areas, however. Figure 5-11 provides a guide to help you decide which type of crowdfunding website to solicit.

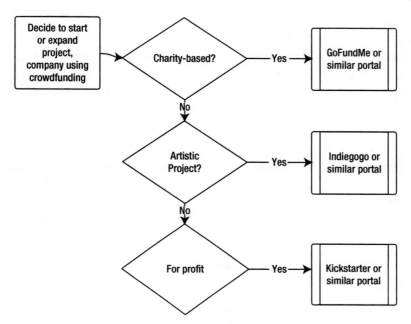

Figure 5-11. Crowdfunding website selection decision chart.

Assuming you have now separated your personal financial needs from your business financing needs, it is time to discuss how to crowdfund for a business.

How to Crowdfund

Even with the disadvantages noted previously, crowdfunding is still a viable option for many firms. The question then becomes, how do you proceed? Let me note a few things:

1. Rules governing the industry have yet to be written. As the SEC noted, they have yet to "write rules to implement the crowdfunding provisions of the JOBS Act. Until the SEC has completed this rulemaking, you cannot act as a crowdfunding intermediary, even if you are already a registered broker. The Division of Corporation Finance also has reminded issuers that any offers or sales of securities purporting to rely on the crowdfunding exemption would be unlawful under the federal securities laws until the SEC's rulemaking is complete."[5]

---

[5] Available at: www.sec.gov/divisions/marketreg/tmjobsact-crowdfundingintermediariesfaq. htm

> ▨ **Note**   There is no substitute for a crowdfunding effort that is honest, compelling, and authentic. Combined with the sense of fulfillment your investors will get from actually seeing their dollars go to a deserving individual (you), and not a bureaucratic organization, your campaign will have a better chance of succeeding. And remember, as with any effort—as long as it's authentic—marketing and publicity can make the difference.

In other words, as of this writing, an SEC-approved website where you can legally issue equity (stock) to nonaccredited investors to fund your small business in the United States does not exist. Still, it never hurts to think early, often, and carefully about the issues and the opportunity. Eventually, several will exist. We provide updates, via the future editions of this book, as information becomes available. In addition, there are several websites that will have current updates related to the JOBS Act, including www.creativeinvest.com and http://crowdfundingnow.blogspot.com.

2. Consider what you are doing. Does the market REALLY exist for your product or service? What makes you special? How complicated is your idea/product/service? Complicated is not necessarily bad; it just means it may be more difficult for the public to understand what you are doing, and consequently, they may not invest right away.

3. Consider your current network. Do you know enough people to get started? As noted earlier, the average GoFundMe user had 482 Facebook friends, and this was sufficient to raise, on average, just over $1,000.00. At the end of the day, crowdfunding is all about the crowd. Do you have one? If not, how quickly can you create one? Will they buy what you are selling?

4. Even if you have a crowd, how will you promote your effort? Will you hire outsiders to do so? Firms are sure to spring up to help. How will you decide whether to use one?

5. What makes you think you can make money doing what you propose to do? Have you "run the numbers"? How much money can you make? How much will it cost to provide the proposed good or service?

6. How will you reward your investors? Is owning a piece of your small company going to be enough?

7. How will you deal with a few thousand "partners?" Email? Newsletter? Facebook? LinkedIn? Dedicated investor website?

8. What other crowdfunding projects have you studied? What worked for them? What didn't?

■ **Note** If you want to succeed with a crowdfunded business, you really need to do your homework. Get a book on starting a business, take a class in entrepreneurship, or work on your business degree. Even though it is easy for people to invest in your business through crowdfunding, that doesn't mean they will. They will be looking very closely to assess your credibility as a business person.

How to Get Started

Many crowdfunding websites currently exist. By the time this book is published, there will be many more. Here's a rundown of those likely to become funding portals under the JOBS Act. Just type the name into Google, and the site will pop right up.

- **Kickstarter.** Launched in 2009 and focused on artistic endeavors, Kickstarter is the best-known crowdfunding platform. According to one source, "13,000 successful campaigns" have raised an average of $5,000 on Kickstarter.

- **Indiegogo.** Online since 2008. Average raised is $15,000 as of November 2011. According to one of the founders, the site is "open to any campaign, any idea, anywhere in the world." Indiegogo recently raised $15 million to create an equity financing platform in keeping with the JOBS Act.

- **MicroVentures.** According to one summary, MicroVentures is "an online broker-dealer that connects startups with more than 1,000 angel investors nationwide looking to make equity investments of $1,000 to $50,000."[6] Average raised: $150,000.

Since enactment, the JOBS Act has spurred the creation of several new crowdfunding websites:

- **PeoplesVC.** I think the venture capital model is outdated and misapplied in the crowdfunding space. Still, some insist on linking crowdfunding to the old model. PeoplesVC is one.

- **Fundable.com.** More consistent with the Kickstarter model. In fact, the website looks like Kickstarter's. Time will

---

[6] Available at: www.inc.com/magazine/201111/comparison-of-crowdfunding-websites.html.

tell about the specific application, but they are off to an early start.

- **WeFunder.** The site claims that "5,397 funders pledge to invest $14,442,100 in startups." Not a bad start.

- **Startup Addict.** This site bills itself as "a community for entrepreneurs, investors & startups."

- **Believers Fund:** A "crowdfunding website for new mobile apps."

- **Rockethub**. This site focuses on artistic projects. One of the key innovations on this site is a sidebar for each project that shows exactly what's going on…in terms of companies getting funded in real time.

- **Quirky.** A crowdfunding website with a focus on products. As noted on the website, "We bring two brand new consumer products to market each week, by enabling a fluid conversation between a global community and Quirky's expert product design staff."

- **New Jelly.** "Focuses on helping artists and films get up off the ground."

- **CoFolio.** Targets local small business firms.

- **Start Some Good.** A crowdfunding website for social entrepreneurs.

- **Peerbackers.** A fairly traditional crowdfunding site.

In addition to these sites, entrepreneurs always have the option of posting their own website or page. But note, you cannot, under the JOBS Act, create your own funding portal to raise money for your venture. You can, however, create a website that points to another website that provides detail on your venture.

Creating a Solicitation

While every crowdfunding website will have specific procedures for soliciting investments, we have outlined some general procedures below. Most sites will want or require these elements.

Known as "the pitch," a solicitation refers to the tools you use to ask for money. A comprehensive pitch has several characteristics:

- The Elevator Speech: a 30 second summary of your product, service, and company. Many suggest the creation of a "high concept" tagline, a sentence or two that gleans the absolute essence of the product or service. I do not. If you can do so, then do so, but some things are more complicated than this. If your effort falls into this category (and think very hard about this), then don't try.

- An all-inclusive description of the problem the business is designed to address. Note: This does not mean you have to build a company around a complicated need. The problem can be as simple as the lack of a good day care facility in your neighborhood, or the fact that your block is missing a good tapas place. You just have to be fully descriptive about the nature of this issue.

- An expansive definition of and a few words on the competition, complete with a full description of how your business will deal with them.

- Under any circumstances, you should be able to briefly and simply describe what you are trying to do. It does not have to be comprehensive, but it must be informative, specific, and allow people to visualize what you are doing.

The Deck

Once you have these items, you are ready to create a ten (not including the cover) slide PowerPoint presentation that describes your business. You will use this to create and supplement your crowdfunding website solicitation. I have included a blank deck in the Appendix.

Contents of the Deck

I suggest the following:

1. Cover slide. Place as much of the information required by the act on this slide as possible. This will include information on the location of the business, the website, email address, and other data.

2. Summary. This is a short, one- to three-sentence statement that presents, in a concise way, what you do or are trying to do. The best summaries are clear, helpful, serious and humorous at the same time, and, again, concise.

3.   Team. This is where you describe the members of your firm. If you aren't working with anyone, that's OK. You just have to explain how you can do what you need to do by yourself, or describe your plan for getting help when you need it.

4.   Problem. What is the nature of the issue you seek to address? Remember, this does not have to be complicated. It can be a simple basic and common problem. You just have to say what it is in a manner that will encourage investors to support you, financially.

5.   Solution. Describe how you will address the issue you identified.

6.   Marketing. Describe, briefly, the size of the market, in local terms if it is a local problem (my day care center will capture 10% of the local day care market) or in national terms if you are selling nationally (my product will generate $X in revenue).

7.   Sales. Now that you have described the problem, the solution, and the market, how will you get your product or service into the hands of people who need it?

8.   Competition. Who else provides the goods or services that you do (or are planning to do)?

9.   Goals. Look at the next three or four calendar quarters (every three months). Describe what will you accomplish, in terms of making money (or other goals, if you won't make money that soon).

10.   Financing. How much money do you need?

Here is what this sequence says,

"Look, there is this problem. We have a team of one or more people to address this problem. We are going to provide a solution to this specific issue in this specific way to these specific people. We will make this much money. Isn't this great? Don't you want to be a part of the solution? Well, by investing this much money, you can."

This approach works is because it is, at once, flexible, general and specific to your venture. You could be discussing a day care center, a hair salon, a biotechnology firm, anything. It's all in how you summarize.

Summary

Crowdfunding has the potential to significantly increase the amount of capital flowing to small firms, known in the act as EGCs. It also has the potential to damage those firms, by subjecting them to burdensome and onerous reporting requirements.

To be successful at crowdfunding requires major effort and deep thought concerning the business venture proposed. Who are you? Where are you? Who owns your business now? Do you mind giving up a portion of your business to people you don't know? What do you bring to the table? Can you convince a group of strangers to give you money for what will be, in many cases, an unproven business venture? Should you try?

If you can't answer these questions, then you may want to think a little more about your business. Talk it over with trusted friends and family. Taking a free business class would not be a bad thing to do even if you can answer the questions. (Google business startup class or go to Yahoo Small Business Advisor, online at http://smallbusiness.yahoo.com/advisor/.) You may want to partner with someone. You may even want to drop the whole thing. But, if you've come this far, I don't think you will.

Portals
Working with Your Partner

In order to crowdfund, you need a portal. In this chapter, I expand on the JOBS Act rules governing these critical entities.

What Is a Portal?

A crowdfunding portal, or funding platform, is an intermediary that stands between an entrepreneur or business owner seeking money and the people with the money. Note that while Indiegogo and Kickstarter are both portals, they are not JOBS Act Portals, since they do not broker equity shares in companies (yet).

A portal can take any organizational form. You can create a portal as an individual, cooperative, partnership, LLC, or corporation.

In whatever form, a portal must register with the SEC as either a broker or a funding portal (as defined in section 3(a)(80) of the Securities Exchange Act of 1934, included in the Appendix to this book). A portal must also register with the securities industry's sole regulatory agency, FINRA.

Funding platforms or portals are websites created for the sale of EGC securities. By law, they have four and only four responsibilities. They must:

- Register with the SEC and FINRA.
- Provide risk and investor education materials.
- Ensure that investors understand risk
- Manage crowdfunding process

Table 6-1 shows the regulatory options for funding portals.

Table 6-1. Rules for Becoming a Portal

Registration:	Broker /Dealer (B/D)	Non–Broker/Dealer (nB/D)
	SEC Broker/Dealer rules apply	SEC Broker/Dealer rules do not apply.
Must:	Be registered with the SEC as a Broker/Dealer	Although not registered as a B/D, non-B/Ds remain under SEC jurisdiction.
		Be a member of a national securities association registered under section 15A. The Financial Industry Regulatory Authority (FINRA) is currently the only registered national securities association.
Enforcement:	SEC/FINRA rules concerning Broker/Dealers	Only FINRA rules written specifically for registered funding portals.
Cannot:		(A) Offer investment advice or recommendations;
		(B) Solicit purchases, sales, or offers to buy the securities offered or displayed on its website or portal;
		(C) Compensate employees, agents, or other persons for such solicitation or based on the sale of securities displayed or referenced on its website or portal;
		(D) Hold, manage, possess, or otherwise handle investor funds or securities; or
		(E) Engage in such other activities as the Commission, by rule, determines appropriate.

■ **Note**   In July 2012, FINRA requested comments on rules they were developing for registered funding portals. According to FINRA, the organization seeks to make sure that the rules written are consistent with both the capital-raising objectives of the JOBS Act and that investors are protected. FINRA requested that commenters describe the requirements "that should apply to registered funding portals, taking into account the relatively limited scope of activities by a registered funding portal permitted under the JOBS Act." In particular, FINRA wants comments about rules regarding general management of crowdfunding websites, risks concerning money laundering, exploitation of the relative position of buyers and sellers, and other concerns. These questions indicate how new this sector is and how unfamiliar industry regulators are with its potential. By the time this book is published, these rules will be likely be written.

Responsibilities of Portals

Portals have a number of critical responsibilities. They must provide investor education and risk disclosures, subject to a review by the SEC to determine the appropriateness of both investor education and risk disclosures. Table 6-2 shows the four responsibilities funding portals have.

Table 6-2. Responsibilities of Funding Portals

Education:	Investor education concerning:
	Risk
	Liquidity
Privacy:	Must protect investor data
Monitor investment limits:	Net worth less than $100,000: greater of $2,000 or 5% of annual income or net worth
	Net worth more than $100,000: 10% of annual income or net worth, up to a maximum of $100,000
EGC:	Review background, including name, legal status, physical address, and website address of EGC issuers.
	Make sure EGCs do not get funding if they do not reach funding goal.
	Make sure portal directors, officers, or partners do not have a financial interest in any EGC issuer using the portal.

Portals have to ensure that investors not only understand they risk losing their entire investment in an EGC stock issue, but they also have to verify that these investors can afford to do so. That's right—portals must make sure that investors affirm that they can afford to lose their entire investment in a crowdfunding issuer.

To determine this, portals will have to question and quiz EGC investors. EGC investors will have to demonstrate their level of understanding concerning the riskiness of investments in EGCs and small companies.

▓ **Note**   If you are considering an EGC investment, you can get a head start on educating yourself about risks in this sector. Look at the State of Wisconsin Department of Financial Institutions' A Consumer's Guide to Small Business Investments online at www.wdfi.org/ymm/sbic/brochures/small_business_investment.htm.

EGC investors will also have to demonstrate an understanding of liquidity, defined as the ability to quickly turn an asset into cash. EGC shares are assumed to be illiquid, so if it turns out that investors need the cash invested back quickly, say, one month after buying an EGC's shares, too bad. They may be locked in to the EGC investment for at least a year. I say "may" because some are working on portal business models that address this issue, perhaps by taking EGC shares from you in exchange for a short-term loan. As of now, however, you should assume that you will not be able to trade or sell your crowdfunding securities until 2014, for at least one year. (The SEC will not issue regulations allowing securities to be issued until the start of 2013 and you have to hold onto the securities for 12 months, so 2014 is a reasonable date.)

Portals also have a role to play in fraud prevention and reduction. They are responsible for obtaining a "background and securities enforcement regulatory history check on each officer, director, and person holding more than 20 percent of the outstanding equity of every (EGC) issuer."

Recall that, according to the JOBS Act, EGC issuers get investors' money only when they meet or exceed their capital raise target. If, as an EGC you say you want to raise $1,000,000, then to get any money at all, you must do so. You will not be able to have a target of $1,000,000 and get, say, $500,000. Portals are responsible for making sure that this is the case. Of course, the way around this is to set your sights lower. Most EGCs will seek to raise a minimal amount of capital. This may lead to sequential EGC issues, as these firm come back to the crowdfunding marketplace repeatedly. But if as long as they are below the $1 million per year capital raising limit, this should not be an impediment.

Portals must also ensure that investors do not exceed the investment limits outlined in the law. They must protect the privacy of information provided by EGC crowdfunding investors.

In addition, portals cannot pay for leads. They can't buy lists of investors, but must develop an investor database organically. You cannot create a portal to finance companies in which you have any financial interest. As of now, it is unclear how most portals will make money.

■ **Note**   How will portals make money? They will provide services to companies seeking to crowdfund. They may sponsor webinars or publish books and other information on the subject. Some may act as matchmakers, pairing small companies together for a fee. The bottom line is that it is hard to say, but they will figure out a way to make it worth their while as well as yours.

The JOBS Act provides an exemption from registration as a broker/dealer for portals that consent to examination by the SEC, that are a member of the only national securities association, known as FINRA. FINRA is required to develop specific rules for funding portal members.

Funding portals regulated by FINRA only cannot offer investment advice. They cannot say, for example, "Shares in Portal Member X are better than shares in Portal Member Y." They cannot ask you to buy securities listed on their site. They must be perfectly neutral with respect to the relative value between competing EGC issuers. They cannot pay "employees, agents or other persons" or someone else to solicit buyers for the EGC securities listed on their site. Portals cannot hold or manage investor funds or securities.

I noted in Chapter 1 that the JOBS Act limits the ability of a state or governmental subdivision to enforce laws against portals, but the JOBS Act makes clear that state security regulators *can* launch enforcement actions against portals or EGC issuers or other persons claiming a security registration exemption under the JOBS Act if these actions are related to a "law or administrative action of a state in which the principal location of the funding portal is located," or if the law or administrative action is consistent with SEC requirements for funding portals."

The act also clarifies that most states *cannot* require EGC issuers to pay state security registration, or filing fees. States where the EGC is located or states where more than 50% of the EGC issue purchasers reside have the option to impose filing fees, however.

States cannot "enforce any law, rule regulation, or other administrative action against a registered funding portal." States do have the ability to examine and enforce state laws that do not conflict with SEC rules.

A Word of Caution

At last count, there were 450 funding portals, with more being added every day. Choosing a broker or funding portal requires careful thought. Given recent history, we would not be surprised to see "crowdfunding portal scams" become more prevalent. One sure sign will be fees. If someone offers to help you take advantage of crowdfunding now by offering services for which there is a steep fee, you should be on guard. Why? Rules implementing the crowdfunding provisions of the JOBS Act have yet to be approved by the SEC. Someone offering to help you raise money over the Internet in exchange for hefty fees may be looking to take advantage of those who are not fully familiar with the act (hence, this book).

Of course, it may be that the person(s) offering the service are themselves unfamiliar with the act. As you now know, this is a complicated law, full of seemingly contradictory language and other potential pitfalls. You need to be sure that the people helping you are fully familiar with the law. (Ask if they have read this book.)

This is important because of the consequences of a violation of the law. If your crowdfunding offering is not legal, it becomes what is called unregistered. This means it is not compliant with SEC rules and regulations. If this happens, you may be liable for putting forward an illegal security offering. If you have concerns, make sure you consult a lawyer, or call FINRA to see if the broker or funding portal offering the service is registered.

Even if you are successful, other factors come into play. Significantly increasing the number of partners you have may cause you to lose focus. The day-to-day operations of the business may suffer as a result. This may be a risk worth taking, however, especially if you have no other potential source of funding.

A final concern may be the unwillingness of big investors to invest in your firm once you have, say, 65,000 small investors, as Pebble Watch potentially has (if everyone who participated in their campaign had also become an investor in the firm). This is, in reality, of limited concern. Private equity funds and other small business investors will follow the money and adapt their business models to deal with an increased number of very small investors in the companies they buy, if they have to.

Transferring and Trading Crowdfunded Securities

At some point, portals will become facilitators for trading crowdfunding securities. This will be a significantly enhanced set of responsibilities, but there is no requirement in the JOBS Act that portals or funding platforms offer this service.

Rules regarding the transfer or trading crowdfunded securities are, however, outlined and specifically limited by the JOBS Act. Crowdfunded securities must be held for, at minimum, one year from the date of purchase. The JOBS Act allows only four exemptions to that rule. Crowdfunded securities can be transferred if:

- They are transferred to the issuer of the securities;

- They are transferred to an accredited investor;

- They are transferred as part of an SEC registered offering;

- They are transferred to a member of the family of the purchaser; or in connection with the death or divorce of the purchaser or other similar circumstance, in the discretion of the Commission.

Note that any purchaser of crowdfunded securities, meaning a security issued through a crowdfunding portal or funding platform, is exempt from the trading restriction if the security purchaser is on tribal territory "or other lands not subject to State or Federal law," is subject to SEC reporting requirements, or is an investment company.[1]

■ **Note** Most portals will probably develop trading capabilities at some point. But the restrictions noted above will still apply.

This is a huge exemption, since mutual funds, closed-end funds, unit investment trusts, investment advisors, broker/dealers, and public companies are all subject to SEC reporting requirements. These entities will be able to trade crowdfunded securities at will. Members of the general public will not, subject to the five exemptions listed above. This means that there may come a day when "investment companies" dominate the market for crowdfunded securities.

■ **Note** The exemptions for investment companies, broker dealers, and other industry players shows how much power the financial services industry still has in Washington. We can only hope that these institutions will not get in the way of the crowdfunding market.

This exemption creates an enhanced risk of fraud—not from EGCs, but from investment companies. In the search for higher returns and competitive

---

[1] According to the SEC, "an 'investment company' is a company (corporation, business trust, partnership, or limited liability company) that issues securities and is primarily engaged in the business of investing in securities." Available at: www.sec.gov/answers/mfinvco.htm

advantage, an investment company or group of investment companies may facilitate the creation of fraudulent "crowdfunded" securities. They would then seek to create demand for these securities by trading them among themselves at ever higher prices, finally allowing the general public in right before prices fall to reflect actual (much lower) value.

Such a scheme might work as follows. Investment Company A buys crowdfunded Security 1 for $10. It arranges for Investment Company B to buy the crowdfunded Security 1 for $20, with a promise that Investment Company A will, at some later point, buy new crowdfunded Security 2 from Investment Company B at an inflated price. Investment Company B gets Investment Company C to buy crowdfunded Security 1 for $30, with a similar promise. Investment Company C sells crowdfunded Security 1 to members of the public for $40. Crowdfunded Security 1 is, however, worth only $10. The public eventually takes the loss.

As of this writing, it looks like the only people who will not be able to trade crowdfunded securities before the year-long holding period is over are the people who need the ability to do so—low- and middle-income investors.

A Tale of Two Portals

At the time this book is being written, Kickstarter and Indiegogo are the two most widely recognized crowdfunding portals. They have fundamentally different views on the future of equity crowdfunding. Indiegogo recently raised $15 million in additional capital so that they can move swiftly into equity crowdfunding.[2] Kickstarter has taken the opposite path, and has said that they will not participate in the equity crowdfunding market.[3]

Their experience should be useful to anyone looking at the crowdfunding experience as a guide for how finding investors through a portal might work.

Kickstarter

Kickstarter is a venture-capital–backed website that facilitates the provision of financing for creative projects. Funding for projects on the site is provided

---

[2] Colleen Taylor, "Indiegogo Raises $15 Million Series A to Make Crowdfunding Go Mainstream," *TechCrunch*, June 6, 2012. Available at: http://techcrunch.com/2012/06/06/indiegogo-funding-15-million-crowdfunding/.

[3] **Om:** With the JOBS Act, there is a lot of talk about Kickstarter being used for crowdfunding of startups, etc. What do you make of all that talk?
Perry: Some people have made assumptions about what we would do. We're not interested in that model. Available at: http://gigaom.com/2012/05/22/kickstarter-founder-perry-chen-intervie/.

by the general public. Three people—Perry Chen, Yancey Strickler, and Charles Adler—created the site in 2008. On June 22, 2012, Kickstarter began publishing statistics about projects hosted on the site. The table below provides summary statistics as on June 23, 2012. (Keep in mind that a project must meet its funding goals to move forward.)

Table 6-3. Kickstarter.com Statistics

Kickstarter						
Total Projects and Dollars						
Launched	**Total dollars**	**Successful dollars**	**Unsuccessful dollars**	**Live dollars 6/23/12**	**Live projects 6/23/12**	**Success rate**
61,054	$263,000,000	$220,000,000	$27,000,000	$16,000,000	4,118	44.05%
Successfully Funded Projects						
Number	**Less than $1K**	**$1 to $10K**	**$10K to $20K**	**$20K to $99K**	**$100K to $999K**	**Over $1 mil**
25,079	3,036	17,405	2,897	1,573	161	7
100%	12.11%	69.40%	11.55%	6.27%	0.64%	0.03%
Unsuccessfully Funded Projects						
	0% funded	**1% to 20% funded**	**21% to 40% funded**	**41% to 60% funded**	**61% to 80% funded**	**81% to 99% funded**
31,857	7,161	19,347	3,562	1,243	380	164
100%	22.48%	60.73%	11.18%	3.90%	1.19%	0.51%

Data as of Saturday 1:10 a.m. EDT June 23, 2012. Source: www.kickstarter.com/help/stats.

By any stretch of the imagination, this is a remarkable track record. The site has facilitated the collection and distribution of $220 million in contributions for over 25,000 projects. Four out of every ten projects launched on the site experienced success. In other words, they raised the capital sought.

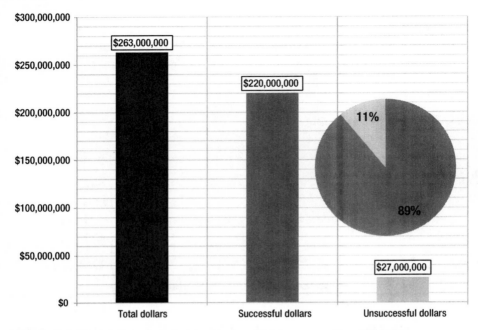

Figure 6-1. Total dollars pledged to projects on Kickstarter as of June 23, 2012.

Seven of ten successful projects were in the $1,000 to $10,000 range, an admittedly wide, but nonetheless impressive, range. Even more interesting, 18% of successful projects sought and received more than $10,000.

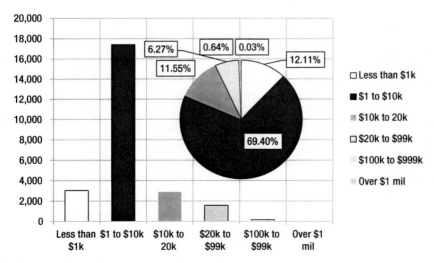

Figure 6-2. Funded projects on Kickstarter as of June 23, 2012.

Over 31,000 projects were not funded. What is important to note is this: The majority, 60%, of these projects never reached the 20% funded level, meaning that potential contributors seem to know early on if a project is a good deal. We believe this reflects "the wisdom of the crowd" and have every reason to believe this wisdom will carry over into the JOBS Act equity funding marketplace.

The lesson here is clear: If you want to be successful at crowdfunding, at least for now, it is important to bring enough of your friends and family along to immediately reach at least 20% of your funding goal. So, if you are looking for $10,000, make sure you have pledges for $2,000. And please note the following: Putting in $2K of your own money will not help. The crowdfunding community will want to see a lot of little investments from a large number of people. This will give confidence to others that you at least have some community support to start with.

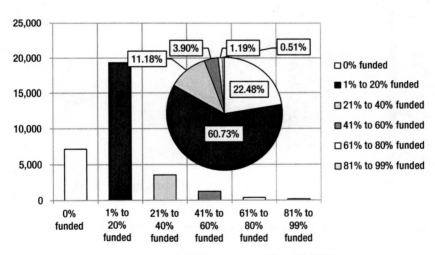

Figure 6-3. Unfunded Projects on Kickstarter as of June 23, 2012.

Indiegogo

The second of the two largest crowdfunding websites currently operational, Indiegogo, seems to have a different focus. It is a softer, more cause-related website than Kickstarter, which seems to have more commercially viable projects on its site.

Started in 2008 by Danae Ringelmann, Slava Rubin, and Eric Schell, and headquartered in San Francisco, California, Indiegogo has as of 2012, "hosted over 100,000 funding campaigns in areas such as music, charity, small business and film."

As of the time of this writing, the site has garnered significant attention and positive feedback for its campaign to raise funds for an elderly school bus monitor, Karen Klein, after a video surfaced showing the woman being brutally and mercilessly harassed by schoolchildren. As of July 10, 2012, the campaign raised $680,354 for her, most of it in the first 48 hours (Figure 6-4).

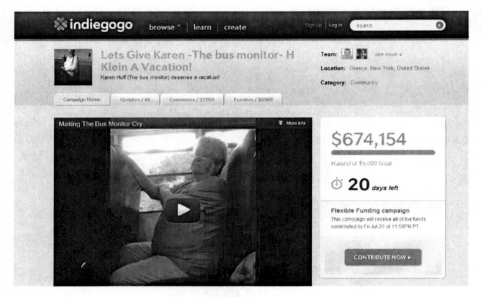

Figure 6-4. Campaign for Karen Klein on Indiegogo.

If you are planning an arts-related, cause-sensitive company, Indiegogo may be the place to start, for now.

This is an example of the power of this medium.

Summary

Portals are intermediaries in crowdfunding transactions. They must register with the SEC and one or more self-regulatory organizations, like FINRA. The JOBS Act mandates portals provide education, specifically on the risks of investing in securities via crowdfunding. Investors must certify, and portals must confirm they understand the risk of investing in EGCs.

Portals manage the EGC investing process, seeking to reduce the risk of fraud and ensuring that EGCs do not receive funds raised until the crowdfunding campaign meets stated dollar-financing goals. They must ensure that portal directors, officers, and partners do not have a financial interest in EGCs seeking financing.

News reports[4] have indicated that there are over 450 crowdfunding platforms. Many more will have launched by the time you read this.

Successful portals exhibit a certain authenticity and transparency. The Klein campaign, noted earlier, is an example of a level of authenticity that is unmistakable. The release, by Kickstarter, of its performance statistics is also an example of transparency that we believe will become a crowdfunding industry standard.

---

[4] "Raising Capital Online: The New Thundering Herd," *The Economist*, June 18, 2012.

The JOBS Act, by Title

Below, you will find the act by title, or section, along with some comments and observations.

An Act of Congress, probably in reference to or short for an action that Congress took, is the starting point for the laws that govern the country. Most acts either require something, prohibit or deny something, or suggest something that should be done.

Acts tend to be broken into titles, or sections of the law. Each section (called a *Title*) typically concerns a given subject. In this case, the titles focus on various parts of the small company capital raising process. Each title seeks to reform or repair a given part of the process. Here are the titles that make up the JOBS Act:

Title I: Reopening American Capital Markets to Emerging Growth Companies

Title II: Access to Capital for Job Creators

Title III: Crowdfunding

Title IV: Small Company Capital Formation

Title V: Private Company Flexibility and Growth

Title VI: Capital Expansion

Title VII: Outreach

The SEC must now create rules and regulations that implement and activate the law outlined in these sections. This is where the rubber meets the road. These regulations, these rules, will govern how the law will accomplish the objectives Congress had in mind when it created the legislation. These rules will be of intense interest to those of us who feel this law has the potential to revive positively business activity in the United States.

For most people, there are two key points to keep in mind. The law allows the SEC to prohibit certain financial institutions and broker/dealers from participating in the crowdfunding market as portals. If the SEC limits participation to firms that have not been cited or fined for prior significant marketplace fraud, then it is my opinion that the crowdfunding market created by the JOBS Act will have a chance to develop fairly. If not, if you see firms that have been fined hundreds of millions of dollars for fraudulent activity participating in the crowdfunding marketplace as portals, I would be concerned. Watch who is allowed to participate. Even if firms that have violated ethical rules of behavior are allowed to participate, try to work with the new players, like Kickstarter, Indiegogo, and others.

Title I

Reopening American Capital Markets to Emerging Growth Companies

This section of the JOBS Act sets the stage for all that comes later. It defines an "Emerging Growth Company" as a security issuer with less than $1 billion in revenue in the most recently completed fiscal (as opposed to calendar) year. It also states that any company with less than a billion in revenue that issued common stock prior to December 8, 2011 is not eligible to be treated as an emerging growth company. Certain disclosure requirements are lifted. The "firewall," or limitations between security issuance activities (underwriting) and research, is lifted for EGCs.

Title I[1]

Sec. 101. Definitions.

Sec. 102. Disclosure obligations.

Sec. 103. Internal controls audit.

Sec. 104. Auditing standards.

Sec. 105. Availability of information about emerging growth companies.

Sec. 106. Other matters.

Sec. 107. Opt-in right for emerging growth companies.

---

[1] Note: Here and through Chapter 13, direct excerpts from the law are presented in a different typeface, Times New Roman. Anything in a different typeface, or set apart from the text, is the author's commentary.

TITLE I—REOPENING AMERICAN CAPITAL MARKETS TO EMERGING GROWTH COMPANIES

SEC. 101. DEFINITIONS.

Definition of Emerging Growth Company (EGC)

(a) SECURITIES ACT OF 1933.—Section 2(a) of the Securities Act of 1933 (15 U.S.C. 77b(a)) is amended by adding at the end the following:"(19) The term 'emerging growth company' means an issuer that had total annual gross revenues of less than $1,000,000,000 (as such amount is indexed for inflation every 5 years by the Commission to reflect the change in the Consumer Price Index for All Urban Consumers published by the Bureau of Labor Statistics, setting the threshold to the nearest 1,000,000) during its most recently completed fiscal year.

Indexes EGC revenue to inflation: EGC revenue limit will increase from $1 billion to a higher dollar amount, assuming positive inflation, or assuming the value of a dollar falls over time.

An issuer that is an emerging growth company as of the first day of that fiscal year shall continue to be deemed an emerging growth company until the earliest of—

"(A) the last day of the fiscal year of the issuer during which it had total annual gross revenues of $1,000,000,000 (as such amount is indexed for inflation every 5 years by the Commission to reflect the change in the Consumer Price Index for All Urban Consumers published by the Bureau of Labor Statistics, setting the threshold to the nearest 1,000,000) or more;

"(B) the last day of the fiscal year of the issuer following the fifth anniversary of the date of the first sale of common equity securities of the issuer pursuant to an effective registration statement under this title;

Sets time and other limits on EGC definition.

"(C) the date on which such issuer has, during the previous 3-year period, issued more than $1,000,000,000 in non-convertible debt; or

"(D) the date on which such issuer is deemed to be a 'large accelerated filer', as defined in section 240.12b–2 of title 17, Code of Federal Regulations, or any successor thereto.".

(b) SECURITIES EXCHANGE ACT OF 1934.—Section 3(a) of the Securities Exchange Act of 1934 (15 U.S.C. 78c(a)) is amended—

(1) by redesignating paragraph (77), as added by section 941(a) of the Investor Protection and Securities Reform Act of 2010 (Public Law 111–203, 124 Stat. 1890), as paragraph (79); and

(2) by adding at the end the following:

"(80) EMERGING GROWTH COMPANY.—The term 'emerging growth company' means an issuer that had total annual gross revenues of less than $1,000,000,000 (as such amount is indexed for inflation every 5 years by the Commission to reflect the change in the Consumer Price Index for All Urban Consumers published by the Bureau of Labor Statistics, setting the threshold to the nearest 1,000,000) during its most recently completed fiscal year. An issuer that is an emerging growth company as of the first day of that fiscal year shall continue to be deemed an emerging growth company until the earliest of—

"(A) the last day of the fiscal year of the issuer during which it had total annual gross revenues of $1,000,000,000 (as such amount is indexed for inflation every 5 years by the Commission to reflect the change in the Consumer Price Index for All Urban Consumers published by the Bureau of Labor Statistics, setting the threshold to the nearest 1,000,000) or more;

"(B) the last day of the fiscal year of the issuer following the fifth anniversary of the date of the first sale of common equity securities of the issuer pursuant to an effective registration statement under the Securities Act of 1933;

"(C) the date on which such issuer has, during the previous 3-year period, issued more than $1,000,000,000 in non-convertible debt; or

"(D) the date on which such issuer is deemed to be a 'large accelerated filer', as defined in section 240.12b–2 of title 17, Code of Federal Regulations, or any successor thereto.".

(c) OTHER DEFINITIONS.—As used in this title, the following definitions shall apply:

(1) COMMISSION.—The term "Commission" means the Securities and Exchange Commission.

(2) INITIAL PUBLIC OFFERING DATE.—The term "initial public offering date" means the date of the first sale of common equity securities of an issuer pursuant to an effective registration statement under the Securities Act of 1933.

(d) EFFECTIVE DATE.—Notwithstanding section 2(a)(19) of the Securities Act of 1933 and section 3(a)(80) of the Securities Exchange Act of 1934, an issuer shall not be an emerging growth company for purposes of such Acts if the first sale of common equity securities of such issuer pursuant to an effective registration statement under the Securities Act of 1933 occurred on or before December 8, 2011.

▨ **Things to notice** The "emerging growth company" definition is the key innovation of Title I. EGC revenues are measured under standard generally accepted accounting principles. Foreign issuers must convert their revenues to dollars, using the foreign currency to dollar rate existing on the last day of the EGC issuers' fiscal year, to determine where they fall along the $1 billion dollar limit. Once you determine that you meet the requirements to be called an EGC, the SEC mandates that a company identify itself as such on the front page of its offering document, or prospectus.

SEC. 102. DISCLOSURE OBLIGATIONS.

(a) EXECUTIVE COMPENSATION.—

(1) EXEMPTION.—Section 14A(e) of the Securities Exchange Act of 1934 (15 U.S.C. 78n–1(e)) is amended—

(A) by striking "The Commission may" and inserting the following:

"(1) IN GENERAL.—The Commission may";

(B) by striking "an issuer" and inserting "any other issuer"; and

(C) by adding at the end the following:

"(2) TREATMENT OF EMERGING GROWTH COMPANIES.—

"(A) IN GENERAL.—An emerging growth company shall be exempt from the requirements of subsections (a) and (b).

"(B) COMPLIANCE AFTER TERMINATION OF EMERGING GROWTH COMPANY TREATMENT.—An issuer that was an emerging growth company but is no longer an emerging growth company shall include the first separate resolution described under subsection (a)(1) not later than the end of—

"(i) in the case of an issuer that was an emerging growth company for less than 2 years after the date of first sale of common equity securities of the issuer pursuant to an effective registration statement under the Securities Act of 1933, the 3-year period beginning on such date; and

"(ii) in the case of any other issuer, the 1-year period beginning on the date the issuer is no longer an emerging growth company.".

(2) PROXIES.—Section 14(i) of the Securities Exchange Act of 1934 (15 U.S.C. 78n(i)) is amended by inserting ", for any issuer other than an emerging growth company," after "including".

(3) COMPENSATION DISCLOSURES.—Section 953(b)(1) of the Investor Protection and Securities Reform Act of 2010 (Public Law 111–203; 124 Stat. 1904) is amended by inserting ", other than an emerging growth company, as that term is defined in section 3(a) of the Securities Exchange Act of 1934," after "require each issuer".

Exempts EGCs from having to seek shareholder approval of executive compensation as required by Dodd/Frank.

(b) FINANCIAL DISCLOSURES AND ACCOUNTING PRONOUNCEMENTS.—

(1) SECURITIES ACT OF 1933.—Section 7(a) of the Securities Act of 1933 (15 U.S.C. 77g(a)) is amended—

(A) by striking "(a) The registration" and inserting the following:

"(a) INFORMATION REQUIRED IN REGISTRATION STATEMENT.—

"(1) IN GENERAL.—The registration"; and (B) by adding at the end the following:

"(2) TREATMENT OF EMERGING GROWTH COMPANIES.—An emerging growth company—

"(A) need not present more than 2 years of audited financial statements in order for the registration statement of such emerging growth company with respect to an initial public offering of its common equity securities to be effective, and in any other registration statement to be filed with the Commission, an emerging growth company need not present selected financial data in accordance with section 229.301 of title 17, Code of Federal Regulations, for any period prior to the earliest audited period presented in connection with its initial public offering; and

Amends the Securities Act of 1933 to allow EGCs to present up to two years of financial data. Prior requirement was for three years of data.

"(B) may not be required to comply with any new or revised financial accounting standard until such date that a company that is not an issuer (as defined under section 2(a) of the Sarbanes-Oxley Act of 2002 (15 U.S.C. 7201(a))) is required to comply with such new or revised accounting standard, if such standard applies to companies that are not issuers.".

(2) SECURITIES EXCHANGE ACT OF 1934.—Section 13(a) of the Securities Exchange Act of 1934 (15 U.S.C. 78m(a)) is amended by adding at the end the following: "In any registration statement, periodic report, or

other reports to be filed with the Commission, an emerging growth company need not present selected financial data in accordance with section 229.301 of title 17, Code of Federal Regulations, for any period prior to the earliest audited period presented in connection with its first registration statement that became effective under this Act or the Securities Act of 1933 and, with respect to any such statement or reports, an emerging growth company may not be required to comply with any new or revised financial accounting standard until such date that a company that is not an issuer (as defined under section 2(a) of the Sarbanes-Oxley Act of 2002 (15 U.S.C. 7201(a))) is required to comply with such new or revised accounting standard, if such standard applies to companies that are not issuers."

(c) OTHER DISCLOSURES.—An emerging growth company may comply with section 229.303(a) of title 17, Code of Federal Regulations, or any successor thereto, by providing information required by such section with respect to the financial statements of the emerging growth company for each period presented pursuant to section 7(a) of the Securities Act of 1933 (15 U.S.C. 77g(a)). An emerging growth company may comply with section 229.402 of title 17, Code of Federal Regulations, or any successor thereto, by disclosing the same information as any issuer with a market value of outstanding voting and nonvoting common equity held by non-affiliates of less than $75,000,000.

Things to notice   Section 102 allows EGCs to reduce the amount of financial data they present to potential investors. This reduced data set includes exemption from reporting certain executive compensation data items. In addition, Sections 103 and 104 establish that EGCs do not need to change auditors or have them attest to the integrity of the EGCs accounting policies and procedures.

SEC. 103. INTERNAL CONTROLS AUDIT.

Section 404(b) of the Sarbanes-Oxley Act of 2002 (15 U.S.C. 7262(b)) is amended by inserting ", other than an issuer that is an emerging growth company (as defined in section 3 of the Securities Exchange Act of 1934)," before "shall attest to".

SEC. 104. AUDITING STANDARDS.

Section 103(a)(3) of the Sarbanes-Oxley Act of 2002 (15 U.S.C. 7213(a)(3)) is amended by adding at the end the following:

"(C) TRANSITION PERIOD FOR EMERGING GROWTH COMPANIES.—

Any rules of the Board requiring mandatory audit firm rotation or a supplement to the auditor's report in which the auditor would be required to provide additional information about the audit and the financial statements of the issuer (auditor discussion and analysis) shall not apply to an audit of an emerging growth company, as defined in section 3 of the Securities Exchange Act of

Exempts EGCs from mandatory audit firm rotation requirements.

1934. Any additional rules adopted by the Board after the date of enactment of this subparagraph shall not apply to an audit of any emerging growth company, unless the Commission determines that the application of such additional requirements is necessary or appropriate in the public interest, after considering the protection of investors and whether the action will promote efficiency, competition, and capital formation.".

SEC. 105. AVAILABILITY OF INFORMATION ABOUT EMERGING GROWTH COMPANIES.

(a) PROVISION OF RESEARCH.—Section 2(a)(3) of the Securities Act of 1933 (15 U.S.C. 77b(a)(3)) is amended by adding at the end the following: "The publication or distribution by a broker or dealer of a research report about an emerging growth company that is the subject of a proposed public offering of the common equity securities of such emerging growth company pursuant to a registration statement that the issuer proposes to file, or has filed, or that is effective shall be deemed for purposes of paragraph (10) of this subsection and section 5(c) not to constitute an offer for sale or offer to sell a security, even if the broker or dealer is participating or

Mandates that the verbal, hard copy or electronic publication and distribution, by a broker/ dealer, of a research report on an EGC, does not constitute an offer to sell a security.

will participate in the registered offering of the securities of the issuer. As used in this paragraph, the term 'research report' means a written, electronic, or oral communication that includes information, opinions, or recommendations with respect to securities of an issuer or an analysis of a security or an issuer, whether or not it provides information reasonably sufficient upon which to base an investment decision.".

(b) SECURITIES ANALYST COMMUNICATIONS.—Section 15D of the Securities Exchange Act of 1934 (15 U.S.C. 78o–6) is amended—

(1) by redesignating subsection (c) as subsection (d); and (2) by inserting after subsection (b) the following:

"(c)   LIMITATION.—Notwithstanding subsection (a) or any other provision of law, neither the Commission nor any national securities association registered under section 15A may adopt or maintain any rule or regulation in connection with an initial public offering of the common equity of an emerging growth company—

> *Disallows the imposition of functional role-based conflict of interest rules with respect to the issuance of common stock by an EGC. Allows EGCs or persons representing an EGC to communicate with accredited investors to "test the waters" or determine level of interest in EGC offering.*

"(1) restricting, based on functional role, which associated persons of a broker, dealer, or member of a national securities association, may arrange for communications between a securities analyst and a potential investor; or

"(2) restricting a securities analyst from participating in any communications with the management of an emerging growth company that is also attended by any other associated person of a broker, dealer, or member of a national securities association whose functional role is other than as a securities analyst.".

(c) EXPANDING PERMISSIBLE COMMUNICATIONS.—Section 5 of the Securities Act of 1933 (15 U.S.C. 77e) is amended—

(1) by redesignating subsection (d) as subsection (e); and

(2) by inserting after subsection (c) the following:

"(d) LIMITATION.—Notwithstanding any other provision of this section, an emerging growth company or any person authorized to act on behalf of an emerging growth company may engage in oral or written communications with potential investors that are qualified institutional buyers or institutions that are accredited investors, as such terms are respectively defined in section 230.144A and section 230.501(a) of title 17, Code of Federal Regulations, or any successor thereto, to determine whether such investors might have an interest in a contemplated securities offering, either prior to or following the date of filing of a registration statement with respect to such securities with the Commission, subject to the requirement of subsection (b) (2).".

(d) POST OFFERING COMMUNICATIONS.—Neither the Commission nor any national securities association registered under section 15A of the Securities Exchange Act of 1934 may adopt or maintain any rule or regulation prohibiting any broker, dealer, or member of a national securities association from publishing or distributing any research report or making a public appearance, with respect to the securities of an emerging growth company, either—

Disallows the imposition of rules that prohibit a broker, dealer or member of a national securities association from speaking, writing, or publishing research reports on the securities of EGCs.

(1) within any prescribed period of time following the initial public offering date of the emerging growth company; or

(2) within any prescribed period of time prior to the expiration date of any agreement between the broker, dealer, or member of a national securities association and the emerging growth company or its shareholders that restricts or prohibits the sale of securities held by the emerging growth company or its shareholders after the initial public offering date.

▓ **Things to notice**   Section 105 establishes that research reports on EGCs issued by brokers issuing an EGC's securities do not constitute an offer to sell a security. The section also expands the types of permissible discussions brokers can conduct concerning EGC issuer securities.

SEC. 106. OTHER MATTERS.

(a) DRAFT REGISTRATION STATEMENTS.—Section 6 of the Securities Act of 1933 (15 U.S.C. 77f) is amended by adding at the end the following:

"(e) EMERGING GROWTH COMPANIES.—

"(1) IN GENERAL.—Any emerging growth company, prior to its initial public offering date, may confidentially submit to the Commission a draft registration statement, for confidential nonpublic review by the staff of the Commission prior to public filing, provided that the initial confidential submission and all amendments thereto shall be publicly filed with the Commission not later than 21 days before the date on which the issuer conducts a road show, as such term is defined in section 230.433(h)(4) of title 17, Code of Federal Regulations, or any successor thereto.

Permits an EGC to submit, to the SEC, a confidential, nonpublic draft securities offering registration statement. Sets 21 day pre "road show" time limit.

"(2) CONFIDENTIALITY.—Notwithstanding any other provision of this title, the Commission shall not be compelled to disclose any information provided to or obtained by the Commission pursuant to this subsection. For purposes of section 552 of title 5, United States Code, this subsection shall be considered a statute described in subsection (b)(3)(B) of such section 552. Information described in or obtained pursuant to this subsection shall be deemed to constitute confidential information for purposes of section 24(b)(2) of the Securities Exchange Act of 1934.".

(b) TICK SIZE.—Section 11A(c) of the Securities Exchange Act of 1934 (15 U.S.C. 78k–1(c)) is amended by adding at the end the following new paragraph:

"(6) TICK SIZE.—

"(A) STUDY AND REPORT.—The Commission shall conduct a study examining the transition to trading and quoting securities in one penny increments, also known as decimalization. The study shall examine the impact that decimalization has had on the number of initial public offerings since its implementation relative to the period before its implementation. The study shall also examine the impact that this change has had on liquidity for small and middle capitalization company securities and whether there is sufficient economic incentive to support trading operations in these securities in penny increments. Not later than 90 days after the date of enactment of this paragraph, the Commission shall submit to Congress a report on the findings of the study.

"(B) DESIGNATION.—If the Commission determines that the securities of emerging growth companies should be quoted and traded using a minimum increment of greater than $0.01, the Commission may, by rule not later than 180 days after the date of enactment of this paragraph, designate a minimum increment for the securities of emerging growth companies that is greater than $0.01 but less than $0.10 for use in all quoting and trading of securities in any exchange or other execution venue."

▓ **Things to notice**   Section 106 also mandates that the SEC conduct a study on "tick size." While not entirely irrelevant to the EGC market, we see this as benefitting hedge fund and others engaged in high frequency trading.

SEC. 107. OPT-IN RIGHT FOR EMERGING GROWTH COMPANIES.

(a) IN GENERAL.—With respect to an exemption provided to emerging growth companies under this title, or an amendment made by this title, an emerging growth company may choose to forgo such exemption and instead comply with the requirements that apply to an issuer that is not an emerging growth company.

(b) SPECIAL RULE.—Notwithstanding subsection (a), with respect to the extension of time to comply with new or revised financial accounting standards provided under section 7(a)(2)(B) of the Securities Act of 1933 and section 13(a) of the Securities Exchange Act of 1934, as added by section 102(b), if an emerging growth company chooses to comply with such standards to the same extent that a non-emerging growth company is required to comply with such standards, the emerging growth company—

Allows an EGC to refuse exemptions allowed under the Act. Says EGC must notify the SEC of its choice. Sets terms of this refusal, states that an EGC that refuses cannot go back, must comply with choice for entire period that it is an EGC.

(1) must make such choice at the time the company is first required to file a registration statement, periodic report, or other report with the Commission under section 13 of the Securities Exchange Act of 1934 and notify the Securities and Exchange Commission of such choice;

(2) may not select some standards to comply with in such manner and not others, but must comply with all such standards to the same extent that a non-emerging growth company is required to comply with such standards; and

(3) must continue to comply with such standards to the same extent that a non-emerging growth company is required to comply with such standards for as long as the company remains an emerging growth company.

Things to notice: Section 107 allows EGCs to voluntarily comply with any requirements that apply to a non-EGC issuer. This option is non revocable, that is, once it is selected, the EGC must abide by all requirements.

SEC. 108. REVIEW OF REGULATION S-K.

(a) REVIEW.—The Securities and Exchange Commission shall conduct a review of its Regulation S-K (17 CFR 229.10 et seq.) to—

Mandates that the SEC review Regulation S-K. Seeks to have the SEC update the Regulation concerning the non-financial portions of the registration statement to lower costs and streamline the registration process.

(1) comprehensively analyze the current registration requirements of such regulation; and

(2) determine how such requirements can be updated to modernize and simplify the registration process and reduce the costs

and other burdens associated with these requirements for issuers who are emerging growth companies.

(b) REPORT.—Not later than 180 days after the date of enactment of this title, the Commission shall transmit to Congress a report of the review conducted under subsection (a). The report shall include the specific recommendations of the Commission on how to streamline the registration process in order to make it more efficient and less burdensome for the Commission and for prospective issuers who are emerging growth companies.

▨ **Things to notice**   Regulation S-K is, according to Wikipedia, a "regulation under the US Securities Act of 1933 that lays out reporting requirements for various SEC filings used by public companies."

Analysis

Given the nature of the changes to the IPO marketplace anticipated by the JOBS Act, the changes mandated by Title I—indeed, by the entire Act—will take some time to implement. The SEC must first write rules to do so. These must be completed by 12/31/12. (Go to www.creativeinvest.com for a rundown of the rules on a real-time basis.) Our analysis starts with some basic issues.

The JOBS Act is a response to concerns about the ability of smaller companies to obtain equity financing. Technology, via the Internet, created a new method that can be used to facilitate the provision of capital to new small businesses. The act seeks to formally allow this method.

The JOBS Act responds to a decline in the number of IPOs in the US by opening the door more widely to small companies. It is not a perfect solution, but it is a very good start. One reason why the JOBS Act is not perfect is due to its lack of recognition concerning exactly what caused the IPO crisis to begin with. I believe a decline in the ethical standards of business behavior caused small businesses to seek other forms of financing. The JOBS Act does little to address this core issue, and, in fact, by granting significant EGC and crowdfunding regulatory advantages to existing broker dealers and securities firms, may exacerbate the problem without having the desired effect of increasing small company IPOs.

All is, however, not lost. I believe the "crowd" and the market itself will prevent this from happening. Investors and small companies will gravitate to authentic, transparent portals, as described in Chapter 6. More detail is provided in Chapter 9.

Title II

Access to Capital for Job Creators

To sell securities legally in the United States, the company offering them must register the securities with the U.S. Securities and Exchange Commission. All information concerning the offering has to be presented to investors via a prospectus. A company can bypass this registration requirement via the use of a limited number of exemptions.

Section 201 of the JOBS Act relaxes rules governing how funds can be raised using one of the most important exemptions, Regulation D. Under two Regulation D rules, 505 and 506, exemptions from certain parts of the registration requirements are allowed for companies that sell their securities to accredited investors. Title II of the Act also modifies and eliminates restrictions on general solicitation or advertising, which is important if an issuer is to offer securities over the Internet.

SEC. 201. MODIFICATION OF EXEMPTION.

(a) MODIFICATION OF RULES.—

(1) Not later than 90 days after the date of the enactment of this Act, the Securities and Exchange Commission shall revise its rules issued in section 230.506 of title 17, Code of Federal Regulations, to provide that the prohibition against general solicitation or general advertising contained in section 230.502(c) of such title shall not apply to offers and sales of securities made pursuant to section 230.506, provided that all purchasers of the securities are accredited investors. Such rules shall require the issuer to take reasonable steps to verify that purchasers of the securities are accredited investors, using such methods as determined by the Commission. Section 230.506 of title 17, Code of Federal Regulations, as revised pursuant to this section, shall continue to be treated as a regulation issued under section 4(2) of the Securities Act of 1933 (15 U.S.C. 77d(2)).

> *Requires the SEC to modify rules concerning public securities offerings so that restrictions concerning advertising and solicitation do not apply if all buyers of an offering are accredited investors. Issuers must verify accredited investor status of buyers, however.*

(2) Not later than 90 days after the date of enactment of this Act, the Securities and Exchange Commission shall revise subsection (d)(1) of section 230.144A of title 17, Code of Federal Regulations, to provide that securities sold under such revised exemption may be offered to persons other than qualified institutional buyers, including by means of general solicitation or general advertising, provided that securities are sold only to persons that the seller and any person acting on behalf of the seller reasonably believe is a qualified institutional buyer.

▥ **Things to Notice**   Several provisions of the JOBS Act went into effect immediately. In a hearing before the House Oversight Committee on June 29, 2012, SEC Chairwoman Mary Schapiro told Congress that her Agency would miss the 90-day (July 5, 2012) deadline that requires the SEC to publish rules lifting the general advertising ban for private securities offerings. This is important: The SEC may be sending a signal to Congress that it is too underfunded, too stressed, too lightly staffed to meet these and other deadlines. This could be a political ploy to get more funding, however. We do not know the truth at this point, but the situation bears watching.

(b) CONSISTENCY IN INTERPRETATION.—Section 4 of the Securities Act of 1933 (15 U.S.C. 77d) is amended—

(1) by striking "The provisions of section 5" and inserting

"(a) The provisions of section 5"; and

(2) by adding at the end the following:

"(b) Offers and sales exempt under section 230.506 of title 17, Code of Federal Regulations (as revised pursuant to section 201 of the Jumpstart Our Business Startups Act) shall not be deemed public offerings under the Federal securities laws as a result of general advertising or general solicitation."

(c) EXPLANATION OF EXEMPTION.—Section 4 of the Securities Act of 1933 (15 U.S.C. 77d) is amended—

(1) by striking "The provisions of section 5" and inserting

"(a) The provisions of section 5"; and

(2) by adding at the end the following:

"(b)(1) With respect to securities offered and sold in compliance with Rule 506 of Regulation D under this Act, no person who meets the conditions set forth in paragraph (2) shall be subject to registration as a broker or dealer pursuant to section 15(a)(1) of this title, solely because—

"(A) that person maintains a platform or mechanism that permits the offer, sale, purchase, or negotiation of or with respect to securities, or permits general solicitations, general advertisements, or similar or related activities by issuers of such securities, whether online, in person, or through any other means;

Creates an exemption from broker/dealer registration requirements for persons who would otherwise be subject to broker/dealer registration simply because they (1) maintain a website or platform that permits transactions or advertising of security offerings; (2) invest in these security offerings or (3) provide ancillary services.

"(B) that person or any person associated with that person co-invests in such securities; or

"(C) that person or any person associated with that person provides ancillary services with respect to such securities.

"(2) The exemption provided in paragraph (1) shall apply to any person described in such paragraph if—

"(A) such person and each person associated with that person receives no compensation in connection with the purchase or sale of such security;

"(B) such person and each person associated with that person does not have possession of customer funds or securities in connection with the purchase or sale of such security; and

"(C) such person is not subject to a statutory disqualification as defined in section 3(a)(39) of this title and does not have any person associated with that person subject to such a statutory disqualification.

"(3) For the purposes of this subsection, the term 'ancillary services' means—

"(A) the provision of due diligence services, in connection with the offer, sale, purchase, or negotiation of such security, so long as such services do not include, for separate compensation, investment advice or recommendations to issuers or investors;

and

"(B) the provision of standardized documents to the issuers and investors, so long as such person or entity does not negotiate the terms of the issuance for and on behalf of third parties and issuers are not required to use the standardized documents as a condition of using the service."

Analysis

Section 201 furthers the exemptions of Title I with an eye toward relaxing or reducing prohibitions against advertising to enable the Internet to be used in the sales process. It limits sales to accredited investors, however, and places a new requirement on the books that requires issuers to verify that accredited investors are, in fact, accredited investors.

Section 201 changes rules concerning general advertising and solicitation. It eliminates restrictions on the promotion of securities online. It also provides that accredited investors must have their status as such verified by issuers. It provides a safe harbor for individuals who offer Rule 506 securities online. Finally, it opens the door for providers of support services, such as accountants and lawyers, by stating that these individuals do not have to register as brokers or dealers.

Title III

Crowdfunding

The crowdfunding provision of the JOBS Act gets most of the attention. Section 301 establishes that transactions under $1 million are exempt from certain registration requirements. Note that the act does not specify that only EGCs can use these provisions. The crowdfunding exemption is broadly available to even very large or very old firms.

SEC. 301. SHORT TITLE.

This title may be cited as the "Capital Raising Online While Deterring Fraud and Unethical Non-Disclosure Act of 2012" or the "CROWDFUND Act".

SEC. 302. CROWDFUNDING EXEMPTION.

(a) SECURITIES ACT OF 1933.—Section 4 of the Securities Act of 1933 (15 U.S.C. 77d) is amended by adding at the end the following:

"(6) transactions involving the offer or sale of securities by an issuer (including all entities controlled by or under common control with the issuer), provided that—

> *Establishes $1 million dollar offering limit with respect to crowdfunded securities.*

"(A) the aggregate amount sold to all investors by the issuer, including any amount sold in reliance on the exemption provided under this paragraph during the 12-month period preceding the date of such transaction, is not more than $1,000,000;

"(B) the aggregate amount sold to any investor by an issuer, including any amount sold in reliance on the exemption provided under this paragraph during the 12-month period preceding the date of such transaction, does not exceed—

"(i) the greater of $2,000 or 5 percent of the annual income or net worth of such investor, as applicable, if either the annual income or the net worth of the investor is less than $100,000; and

"(ii) 10 percent of the annual income or net worth of such investor, as applicable, not to exceed a maximum aggregate amount sold of $100,000, if either the annual income or net worth of the investor is equal to or more than $100,000;

"(C) the transaction is conducted through a broker or funding portal that complies with the requirements of section 4A(a); and

Establishes income thresholds for those purchasing crowdfunded securities.

"(D) the issuer complies with the requirements of section 4A(b)."

■ **Things to Notice**   The income limits apply to all transactions through crowdfunding portals. In other words, status as an accredited investor does not allow you to purchase more securities on a crowdfunding portal than nonaccredited investors.

(b) REQUIREMENTS TO QUALIFY FOR CROWDFUNDING EXEMPTION.—

The Securities Act of 1933 (15 U.S.C. 77a et seq.) is amended by inserting after section 4 the following:

"SEC. 4A. REQUIREMENTS WITH RESPECT TO CERTAIN SMALL TRANSACTIONS.

"(a) REQUIREMENTS ON INTERMEDIARIES.—A person acting as an intermediary in a transaction involving the offer or sale of securities for the account of others pursuant to section 4(6) shall—

"(1) register with the Commission as—

"(A) a broker; or

"(B) a funding portal (as defined in section 3(a)(80) of the Securities Exchange Act of 1934);

Establishes registration and other requirements for crowdfunding portals and intermediaries.

"(2) register with any applicable self-regulatory organization (as defined in section 3(a)(26) of the Securities Exchange Act of 1934);

"(3) provide such disclosures, including disclosures related to risks and other investor education materials, as the Commission shall, by rule, determine appropriate;

"(4) ensure that each investor—

"(A) reviews investor-education information, in accordance with standards established by the Commission, by rule;

Establishes that portals must affirm investors understand the risks of crowdfunded small-company investments.

"(B) positively affirms that the investor understands that the investor is risking the loss of the entire investment, and that the investor could bear such a loss; and

"(C) answers questions demonstrating—

"(i) an understanding of the level of risk generally applicable to investments in startups, emerging businesses, and small issuers;

"(ii) an understanding of the risk of illiquidity;

and

"(iii) an understanding of such other matters as the Commission determines appropriate, by rule;

"(5) take such measures to reduce the risk of fraud with respect to such transactions, as established by the Commission, by rule, including obtaining a background and securities enforcement regulatory history check on each officer, director, and person holding more than 20 percent of the outstanding equity of every issuer whose securities are offered by such person;

"(6) not later than 21 days prior to the first day on which securities are sold to any investor (or such other period as the Commission may establish), make available to the Commission and to potential investors any information provided by the issuer pursuant to subsection (b);

"(7) ensure that all offering proceeds are only provided to the issuer when the aggregate capital raised from all investors is equal to or greater than a target offering amount, and allow all investors to cancel their commitments to invest, as the Commission shall, by rule, determine appropriate;

Establishes "all or none" nature of crowdfunding portals under the Act. Issuers must raise all funds sought. Allows investors to cancel.

"(8) make such efforts as the Commission determines appropriate, by rule, to ensure that no investor in a 12-month period has purchased securities offered pursuant to section 4(6) that, in the aggregate, from all issuers, exceed the investment limits set forth in section 4(6)(B);

"(9) take such steps to protect the privacy of information collected from investors as the Commission shall, by rule, determine appropriate;

"(10) not compensate promoters, finders, or lead generators for providing the broker or funding portal with the personal identifying information of any potential investor;

Requires portals to safeguard investor information; prohibits them from buying leads; prohibits portal affiliates from having a financial interest in companies raising funds through their portals.

"(11) prohibit its directors, officers, or partners (or any person occupying a similar status or performing a similar function) from having any financial interest in an issuer using its services; and

"(12) meet such other requirements as the Commission may, by rule, prescribe, for the protection of investors and in the public interest.

"(b) REQUIREMENTS FOR ISSUERS.—For purposes of section 4(6), an issuer who offers or sells securities shall—

"(1) file with the Commission and provide to investors and the relevant broker or funding portal, and make available to potential investors—

"(A) the name, legal status, physical address, and website address of the issuer;

Establishes specific information issuers have to provide to investors.

"(B) the names of the directors and officers (and any persons occupying a similar status or performing a similar function), and each person holding more than 20 percent of the shares of the issuer;

"(C) a description of the business of the issuer and the anticipated business plan of the issuer;

"(D) a description of the financial condition of the issuer, including, for offerings that, together with all other offerings of the issuer under section 4(6) within the preceding 12-month period, have, in the aggregate, target offering amounts of—

Income tax reporting requirements based on amount raised: $100,000 or less: tax returns and self-certified statement.
 $100,000 to $500,000 – CPA-reviewed statements.
$500,000 to $1,000,000 – audited financial statements.

"(i) $100,000 or less—

"(I) the income tax returns filed by the issuer for the most recently completed year (if any); and

"(II) financial statements of the issuer, which shall be certified by the principal executive officer of the issuer to be true and complete in all material respects;

"(ii) more than $100,000, but not more than $500,000, financial statements reviewed by a public accountant who is independent of the issuer, using professional standards and procedures for such review or standards and procedures established by the Commission, by rule, for such purpose; and

"(iii) more than $500,000 (or such other amount as the Commission may establish, by rule), audited financial statements;

"(E) a description of the stated purpose and intended use of the proceeds of the offering sought by the issuer with respect to the target offering amount;

"(F) the target offering amount, the deadline to reach the target offering amount, and regular updates regarding the progress of the issuer in meeting the target offering amount;

"(G) the price to the public of the securities or the method for determining the price, provided that, prior to sale, each investor shall be provided in writing the final price and all required disclosures, with a reasonable opportunity to rescind the commitment to purchase the securities;

"(H) a description of the ownership and capital structure of the issuer, including—

"(i) terms of the securities of the issuer being offered and each other class of security of the issuer, including how such terms may be modified, and a summary of the differences between such securities, including how the rights of the securities being offered may be materially limited, diluted, or qualified by the rights of any other class of security of the issuer; "(ii) a description of how the exercise of the rights held by the principal shareholders of the issuer could negatively impact the purchasers of the securities being offered;

Establishes information that crowdfunding security issuers have to report to investors concerning rights.

▓ **Things to Notice**　For most firms, the description of ownership and exercise rights will be irrelevant. Most firms will have a limited number of owners or shareholders before offering securities for sale.

"(iii) the name and ownership level of each existing shareholder who owns more than 20 percent of any class of the securities of the issuer;

"(iv) how the securities being offered are being valued, and examples of methods for how such securities may be valued by the issuer in the future, including during subsequent corporate actions; and

"(v) the risks to purchasers of the securities relating to minority ownership in the issuer, the risks associated with corporate actions, including additional issuances of shares, a sale of the issuer or of assets of the issuer, or transactions with related parties; and

"(I) such other information as the Commission may, by rule, prescribe, for the protection of investors and in the public interest;

"(2) not advertise the terms of the offering, except for notices which direct investors to the funding portal or broker;

"(3) not compensate or commit to compensate, directly or indirectly, any person to promote its offerings through communication channels provided by a broker or funding portal, without taking such steps as the Commission shall, by rule, require to ensure that such person clearly discloses the receipt, past or prospective, of such compensation, upon each instance of such promotional communication;

"(4) not less than annually, file with the Commission and provide to investors reports of the results of operations and financial statements of the issuer, as the Commission shall, by rule, determine appropriate, subject to such exceptions and termination dates as the Commission may establish, by rule; and

"(5) comply with such other requirements as the Commission may, by rule, prescribe, for the protection of investors and in the public interest.

"(c) LIABILITY FOR MATERIAL MISSTATEMENTS AND OMISSIONS.—

"(1) ACTIONS AUTHORIZED.—

"(A) IN GENERAL.—Subject to paragraph (2), a person who purchases a security in a transaction exempted by the provisions of section 4(6) may bring an action against an issuer described in paragraph (2), either at law or in equity in any court of competent jurisdiction, to recover the consideration paid for such security with interest thereon, less the amount of any income received thereon, upon the tender of such security, or for damages if such person no longer owns the security.

"(B) LIABILITY.—An action brought under this paragraph shall be subject to the provisions of section 12(b) and section 13, as if the liability were created under section 12(a)(2).

"(2) APPLICABILITY.—An issuer shall be liable in an action under paragraph (1), if the issuer—

"(A) by the use of any means or instruments of transportation or communication in interstate commerce or of the mails, by any means of any written or oral communication, in the offering

Establishes legal liability for fraudulent statements made by security issuers.

or sale of a security in a transaction exempted by the provisions of section 4(6), makes an untrue statement of a material fact or omits to state a material fact required to be stated or necessary in order to make the statements, in the light of the circumstances under which they were made, not misleading, provided that the purchaser did not know of such untruth or omission; and

"(B) does not sustain the burden of proof that such issuer did not know, and in the exercise of reasonable care could not have known, of such untruth or omission.

▧ **Note**   I believe the vast majority of firms will accurately represent their operations. There is the potential for legal abuse, however. Some may seek to take innocent statements made by issuers at the start of the fundraising process and make them actionable at some much later point. Statements may also be misused by competitors.

"(3) DEFINITION.—As used in this subsection, the term 'issuer' includes any person who is a director or partner of the issuer, and the principal executive officer or officers, principal financial officer, and controller or principal accounting officer of the issuer (and any person occupying a similar status or performing a similar function) that offers or sells a security in a transaction exempted by the provisions of section 4(6), and any person who offers or sells the security in such offering.

"(d) INFORMATION AVAILABLE TO STATES.—The Commission shall make, or shall cause to be made by the relevant broker or funding portal, the information described in subsection (b) and such other information as the Commission, by rule, determines appropriate, available to the securities commission (or any agency or office performing like functions) of each State and territory of the United States and the District of Columbia.

"(e) RESTRICTIONS ON SALES.—Securities issued pursuant to a transaction described in section 4(6)—

"(1) may not be transferred by the purchaser of such securities during the 1-year period beginning on the date of purchase, unless such securities are transferred—

"(A) to the issuer of the securities;

"(B) to an accredited investor;

"(C) as part of an offering registered with the Commission;

or

"(D) to a member of the family of the purchaser or the equivalent, or in connection with the death or divorce of the purchaser or other similar circumstance, in the discretion of the Commission; and

"(2) shall be subject to such other limitations as the Commission shall, by rule, establish.

Restricts transfers of crowdfunded securities except under four conditions:
1. Transferred to the issuer.
2. Transferred to an accredited investor.
3. Transferred as part of a registered security offering.
4. Transferred to a family member as part of a divorce proceeding or death of the buyer.

"(f) APPLICABILITY.—Section 4(6) shall not apply to transactions involving the offer or sale of securities by any issuer that—

"(1) is not organized under and subject to the laws of a State or territory of the United States or the District of Columbia;

"(2) is subject to the requirement to file reports pursuant to section 13 or section 15(d) of the Securities Exchange Act of 1934;

"(3) is an investment company, as defined in section 3 of the Investment Company Act of 1940, or is excluded from the definition of investment company by section 3(b) or section 3(c) of that Act; or

"(4) the Commission, by rule or regulation, determines appropriate.

"(g) RULE OF CONSTRUCTION.—Nothing in this section or section 4(6) shall be construed as preventing an issuer from raising capital through methods not described under section 4(6).

"(h) CERTAIN CALCULATIONS.—

"(1) DOLLAR AMOUNTS.—Dollar amounts in section 4(6) and subsection (b) of this section shall be adjusted by the Commission not less frequently than once every 5 years, by notice published in the Federal Register to reflect any change in the Consumer Price Index for All Urban Consumers published by the Bureau of Labor Statistics.

"(2) INCOME AND NET WORTH.—The income and net worth of a natural person under section 4(6)(B) shall be calculated in accordance with any rules of the Commission under this title regarding the calculation of the income and net worth, respectively, of an accredited investor."

(c) RULEMAKING.—Not later than 270 days after the date of enactment of this Act, the Securities and Exchange Commission (in this title referred to as the "Commission") shall issue such rules as the Commission determines may be necessary or appropriate for the protection of investors to carry out sections 4(6) and section 4A of the Securities Act of 1933, as added by this title. In carrying out this section, the Commission shall consult with any securities commission (or any agency or office performing like functions) of the States, any territory of the United States, and the District of Columbia, which seeks to consult with the Commission, and with any applicable national securities association.

(d) DISQUALIFICATION.—

(1) IN GENERAL.—Not later than 270 days after the date of enactment of this Act, the Commission shall, by rule, establish disqualification provisions under which—

Requires the SEC to create rules governing the disqualification of issuers, brokers, and portals.

(A) an issuer shall not be eligible to offer securities pursuant to section 4(6) of the Securities Act of 1933, as added by this title; and

(B) a broker or funding portal shall not be eligible to effect or participate in transactions pursuant to that section 4(6).

(2) INCLUSIONS.—Disqualification provisions required by this subsection shall—

(A) be substantially similar to the provisions of section 230.262 of title 17, Code of Federal Regulations (or any successor thereto); and

(B) disqualify any offering or sale of securities by a person that—

(i) is subject to a final order of a State securities commission (or an agency or officer of a State performing like functions), a State authority that supervises or examines banks, savings associations, or credit unions, a State insurance commission (or an agency or officer of a State performing like functions), an appropriate Federal banking agency, or the National Credit Union Administration, that—

(I) bars the person from—

(aa) association with an entity regulated by such commission, authority, agency, or officer;

(bb) engaging in the business of securities, insurance, or banking; or

(cc) engaging in savings association or credit union activities; or

(II) constitutes a final order based on a violation of any law or regulation that prohibits fraudulent, manipulative, or deceptive conduct within the 10-year period ending on the date of the filing of the offer or sale; or

(ii) has been convicted of any felony or misdemeanor in connection with the purchase or sale of any security or involving the making of any false filing with the Commission.

Note I think that brokers fined by the SEC in various cases concerning the violation of securities laws should be excluded from this market. I doubt this will be the case, however.

SEC. 303. EXCLUSION OF CROWDFUNDING INVESTORS FROM SHAREHOLDER CAP.

(a) EXEMPTION.—Section 12(g) of the Securities Exchange Act of 1934 (15 U.S.C. 78l(g)) is amended by adding at the end the following:

"(6) EXCLUSION FOR PERSONS HOLDING CERTAINSECURITIES.—

The Commission shall, by rule, exempt, conditionally or unconditionally, securities acquired pursuant to an offering made under section 4(6) of the Securities Act of 1933 from the provisions of this subsection.".

(b) RULEMAKING.—The Commission shall issue a rule to carry out section 12(g)(6) of the Securities Exchange Act of 1934 (15 U.S.C. 78c), as added by this section, not later than 270 days after the date of enactment of this Act.

SEC. 304. FUNDING PORTAL REGULATION.

(a) EXEMPTION.—

(1) IN GENERAL.—Section 3 of the Securities Exchange Act of 1934 (15 U.S.C. 78c) is amended by adding at the end the following:

"(h) LIMITED EXEMPTION FOR FUNDING PORTALS.—

"(1) IN GENERAL.—The Commission shall, by rule, exempt, conditionally or unconditionally, a registered funding portal from the requirement to register as a broker or dealer under section 15(a)(1), provided that such funding portal—

Requires the SEC to create rules that release funding portals from rules that would otherwise require them to register as broker/dealers, as long as they remain subject to SEC authority.

"(A) remains subject to the examination, enforcement, and other rulemaking authority of the Commission;

"(B) is a member of a national securities association registered under section 15A; and

"(C) is subject to such other requirements under this title as the Commission determines appropriate under such rule.

"(2) NATIONAL SECURITIES ASSOCIATION MEMBERSHIP.—For purposes of sections 15(b)(8) and 15A, the term 'broker or dealer' includes a funding portal and the term 'registered broker or dealer' includes a registered funding portal, except to the extent that the Commission, by rule, determines otherwise, provided that a national securities association shall only examine for and enforce against a registered funding portal rules of such national securities association written specifically for registered funding portals.".

(2) RULEMAKING.—The Commission shall issue a rule to carry out section 3(h) of the Securities Exchange Act of 1934 (15 U.S.C. 78c), as added by this subsection, not later than 270 days after the date of enactment of this Act.

(b) DEFINITION.—Section 3(a) of the Securities Exchange Act of 1934 (15 U.S.C. 78c(a)) is amended by adding at the end the following:

"(80) FUNDING PORTAL.—The term 'funding portal' means any person acting as an intermediary in a transaction involving the offer or sale of securities for the account of others, solely pursuant to section 4(6) of the Securities Act of 1933 (15 U.S.C. 77d(6)), that does not—

"(A) offer investment advice or recommendations;

"(B) solicit purchases, sales, or offers to buy the securities offered or displayed on its website or portal;

"(C) compensate employees, agents, or other persons for such solicitation or based on the sale of securities displayed or referenced on its website or portal;

"(D) hold, manage, possess, or otherwise handle investor funds or securities; or

Limits the ability of states to enforce security registration and offering laws against a funding portal. States and state security regulators do have the authority to enforce laws concerning fraud. In addition, for portals specializing in specific geographic areas, allows states to impose filing fees. Also allows securities regulators in an issuer's home jurisdiction to assess fees.

"(E) engage in such other activities as the Commission, by rule, determines appropriate."

SEC. 305. RELATIONSHIP WITH STATE LAW.

(a) IN GENERAL.—Section 18(b)(4) of the Securities Act of 1933

(15 U.S.C. 77r(b)(4)) is amended—

(1) by redesignating subparagraphs (C) and (D) as subparagraphs (D) and (E), respectively; and

(2) by inserting after subparagraph (B) the following:

"(C) section 4(6);"

(b) CLARIFICATION OF THE PRESERVATION OF STATE ENFORCEMENT AUTHORITY.—

(1) IN GENERAL.—The amendments made by subsection

(a) relate solely to State registration, documentation, and offering requirements, as described under section 18(a) of Securities Act of 1933 (15 U.S.C. 77r(a)), and shall have no impact or limitation on other State authority to take enforcement action with regard to an issuer, funding portal, or any other person or entity using the exemption from registration provided by section 4(6) of that Act.

(2) CLARIFICATION OF STATE JURISDICTION OVER UNLAWFUL CONDUCT OF FUNDING PORTALS AND ISSUERS.—Section 18(c)(1) of the Securities Act of 1933 (15 U.S.C. 77r(c)(1)) is amended by striking "with respect to fraud or deceit, or unlawful conduct by a broker or dealer, in connection with securities or securities transactions." and inserting the following: ", in connection with securities or securities transactions

"(A) with respect to—

"(i) fraud or deceit; or

"(ii) unlawful conduct by a broker or dealer; and

"(B) in connection to a transaction described under section 4(6), with respect to—

"(i) fraud or deceit; or

"(ii) unlawful conduct by a broker, dealer, funding portal, or issuer."

(c) NOTICE FILINGS PERMITTED.—Section 18(c)(2) of the Securities Act of 1933 (15 U.S.C. 77r(c)(2)) is amended by adding at the end the following:

"(F) FEES NOT PERMITTED ON CROWDFUNDED SECURITIES.—

Notwithstanding subparagraphs (A), (B), and (C), no filing or fee may be required with respect to any security that is a covered security pursuant to subsection (b)(4)(B), or will be such a covered security upon completion of the transaction, except for the securities commission (or any agency or office performing like functions) of the State of the principal place of business of the issuer, or any State in which purchasers of 50 percent or greater of the aggregate amount of the issue are residents, provided that for purposes of this subparagraph, the term 'State' includes the District of Columbia and the territories of the United States."

▓ **Note**   This will be a tricky issue for states and localities, since the imposition of significant filing or other fees may defeat the purpose of the law. We expect several states to attempt to impose crowdfunding fees, given the fiscal crisis in many states.

(d) FUNDING PORTALS.—

(1) STATE EXEMPTIONS AND OVERSIGHT.—Section 15(i) of the Securities Exchange Act of 1934 (15 U.S.C. 78o(i)) is amended—

(A) by redesignating paragraphs (2) and (3) as paragraphs (3) and (4), respectively; and

(B) by inserting after paragraph (1) the following:

"(2) FUNDING PORTALS.—

"(A) LIMITATION ON STATE LAWS.—Except as provided in subparagraph (B), no State or political subdivision thereof may enforce any law, rule, regulation, or other administrative action against a registered funding portal with respect to its business as such.

"(B) EXAMINATION AND ENFORCEMENT AUTHORITY.—

Subparagraph (A) does not apply with respect to the examination and enforcement of any law, rule, regulation, or administrative action of a State or political subdivision thereof in which the principal place of business of a registered funding portal is located, provided that such law, rule, regulation, or administrative action is not in addition to or different from the requirements for registered funding portals established by the Commission.

"(C) DEFINITION.—For purposes of this paragraph, the term 'State' includes the District of Columbia and the territories of the United States."

(2) STATE FRAUD AUTHORITY.—Section 18(c)(1) of the Securities Act of 1933 (15 U.S.C. 77r(c)(1)) is amended by striking "or dealer" and inserting ", dealer, or funding portal."

Analysis

Section 302 establishes what a crowdfunding exempt transaction is. It also establishes buying limits for crowdfunding investors: $2,000 or 5% of annual income or net worth for those with less than $100,000 in either and 10% of annual income or net worth, subject to a global maximum of $100,000 for those with a net worth greater than $100,000.

Figure 9-1 shows this in graphical form for persons with incomes and net worth up to $100,000. The axis on the left represents annual income or net worth. This is shown by the gray bars. The right axis shows the total that a person can invest annually. This is represented by the black line. This chart shows one interesting loophole: the language of the law allows someone with no income to invest $2,000 (greater of $2,000 or 5%. 5% of zero is zero. $2,000 is larger than zero).

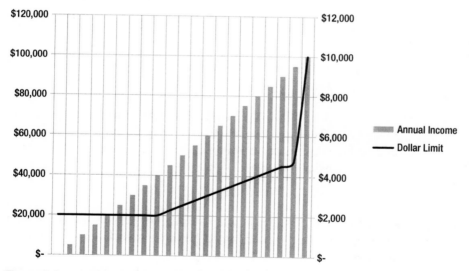

Figure 9-1. Annual income (gray bars, left scale) and crowdfunding investing limits (black line, right scale) for incomes from $0 to $120,000.

Figure 9-2 shows this in graphical form for persons with incomes and net worth greater than $100,000 to $1,100,000. As in Figure 9-1, the axis on the left represents annual income or net worth. This is shown by the gray bars. The right axis shows the total that a person can invest annually, represented by the black line. This chart shows that high net worth investors are well protected by the law. Figure 9-3 combines the data from Figures 9-1 and 9-2.

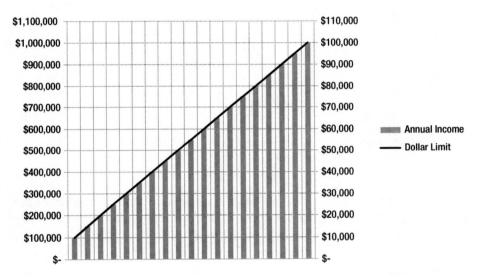

Figure 9-2. Annual income (gray bars, left scale) and crowdfunding investing limits (black line, right scale) for incomes from $100,000 to $1,100,000.

To be effective, transactions must go through a qualified funding portal. The requirements for these are also set out in section 301. The section establishes the education, fraud protection, and privacy requirements of crowdfunding websites. It also establishes the "all or none" aspects of EGC offerings. Section 301 sets prohibitions on compensating those who find investors and establishes the conflict-of-interest prohibition.

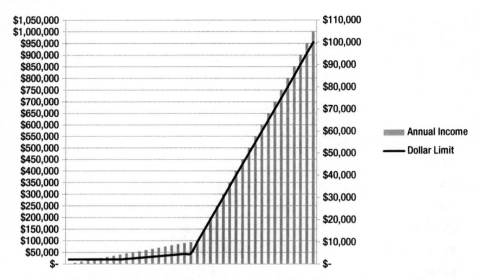

Figure 9-3. Annual income (gray bars, left scale) and crowdfunding investing limits (black line, right scale) for incomes from $0 to $1,050,000.

Requirements for EGC issuers are listed. It establishes that any payments for those who promote a site's offerings through communication channels provided by a broker or funding portal must be clearly disclosed. It also establishes the schedule for filing annual funding portal operating reports with the SEC.

Table 9-1 shows financial statement data required of EGC issuers.

Table 9-1. EGC Financial Statement Requirements, by Amount of Capital Raised

Capital—Amount Raised	EGC Issuer Requirements	Who Certifies Statements
$0 to $100,000	Income tax return	CEO
$100,000 to $500,000	Financial statements	Independent CPA
$500,000 to $1,000,000	Financial statements	Audited

Section 301 of the JOBS Act:

- Establishes liability for misleading statements made by EGC issuers.

- Outlines the conditions regarding the transfer and sale of EGC issues, once bought.

- Mandates that dollar amount limits set out in the section must be adjusted for inflation once every five years.

- Requires that the SEC create rules that determine when an EGC is ineligible to issue securities.

- Establishes that the SEC must exempt EGC crowdfunding securities from section 4(6) of the 33 Act (Section 303).

- Outlines rules for funding portals, establishes the general registration and operating conditions for these entities (Section 304).

- Limits the ability of the SEC to interfere with state security regulators' enforcement or examination of funding portals, establishes that the exemptions granted from state regulation apply only to "registration, documentation and offering requirements" (Section 305).

- Establishes conditions under which state fees can be applied to crowdfunded securities.

CHAPTER

10

Title IV
Small Company Capital Formation

Some have called Title IV the most important part of the JOBS Act, since it expands what are known as Regulation A exemptions. Regulation A allows the SEC to remove registration restrictions from any class of security if it determines that doing so is in the public interest. Securities issued under a Regulation A exemption had been previously limited to $5 million. The JOBS Act raises that limit to $50 million. This is a very large increase, a change we don't normally see.

SEC. 401. AUTHORITY TO EXEMPT CERTAIN SECURITIES.

(a) IN GENERAL.—Section 3(b) of the Securities Act of 1933 (15 U.S.C. 77c(b)) is amended—

(1) by striking "(b) The Commission" and inserting the following:

"(b) ADDITIONAL EXEMPTIONS.—

"(1) SMALL ISSUES EXEMPTIVE AUTHORITY.—The Commission"; and

> Requires the SEC to create a class of securities that are subject to reduced registration requirements.

(2) by adding at the end the following:

"(2) ADDITIONAL ISSUES.—The Commission shall by rule or regulation add a class of securities to the securities exempted pursuant to this section in accordance with the following terms and conditions:

"(A) The aggregate offering amount of all securities offered and sold within the prior 12-month period in reliance on the exemption added in accordance with this paragraph shall not exceed $50,000,000.

"(B) The securities may be offered and sold publicly.

"(C) The securities shall not be restricted securities within the meaning of the Federal securities laws and the regulations promulgated thereunder.

Establishes that the amount of the securities sold in any 12-month period will not exceed $50 million.

"(D) The civil liability provision in section 12(a)(2) shall apply to any person offering or selling such securities.

"(E) The issuer may solicit interest in the offering prior to filing any offering statement, on such terms and conditions as the Commission may prescribe in the public interest or for the protection of investors.

"(F) The Commission shall require the issuer to file audited financial statements with the Commission annually.

Requires an issuer to file audited financial statements.

"(G) Such other terms, conditions, or requirements as the Commission may determine necessary in the public interest and for the protection of investors, which may include—

"(i) a requirement that the issuer prepare and electronically file with the Commission and distribute to prospective investors an offering statement, and any related documents, in such form and with such content as prescribed by the Commission, including audited financial statements, a description of the issuer's business operations, its financial condition, its corporate governance principles, its use of investor funds, and other appropriate matters; and

Requires that offering documents be filed with the SEC electronically, in keeping with the move to using the Internet to facilitate the flow of capital.

"(ii) disqualification provisions under which the exemption shall not be available to the issuer or its predecessors, affiliates, officers, directors, underwriters, or other related persons, which shall be substantially similar to the disqualification provisions contained in the regulations adopted in accordance with section 926 of the Dodd-Frank Wall Street Reform and Consumer Protection Act (15 U.S.C. 77d note).

"(3) LIMITATION.—Only the following types of securities may be exempted under a rule or regulation adopted pursuant to paragraph (2): equity securities, debt securities, and debt securities convertible or exchangeable to equity interests, including any guarantees of such securities.

"(4) PERIODIC DISCLOSURES.—Upon such terms and conditions as the Commission determines necessary in the public interest and for the protection of investors, the Commission by rule or regulation may require an issuer of a class of securities exempted under paragraph (2) to make available to investors and file with the Commission periodic disclosures regarding the issuer, its business operations, its financial condition, its corporate governance principles, its use of investor funds, and other appropriate matters, and also may provide for the suspension and termination of such a requirement with respect to that issuer.

"(5) ADJUSTMENT.—Not later than 2 years after the date of enactment of the Small Company Capital Formation Act of 2011 and every 2 years thereafter, the Commission shall review the offering amount limitation described in paragraph (2)(A) and shall increase such amount as the Commission determines appropriate. If the Commission determines not to increase such amount, it shall report to the Committee on Financial Services of the House of Representatives and the Committee on Banking, Housing, and Urban Affairs of the Senate on its reasons for not increasing the amount."

(b) TREATMENT AS COVERED SECURITIES FOR PURPOSES OF NSMIA.—Section 18(b)(4) of the Securities Act of 1933 (as amended by section 303) (15 U.S.C. 77r(b)(4)) is further amended by inserting after subparagraph (C) (as added by such section) the following:

"(D) a rule or regulation adopted pursuant to section 3(b)(2) and such security is—

"(i) offered or sold on a national securities exchange; or

"(ii) offered or sold to a qualified purchaser, as defined by the Commission pursuant to paragraph (3) with respect to that purchase or sale;".

(c) CONFORMING AMENDMENT.—Section 4(5) of the Securities Act of 1933 is amended by striking "section 3(b)" and inserting "section 3(b)(1)."

SEC. 402. STUDY ON THE IMPACT OF STATE BLUE SKY LAWS ON REGULATION A OFFERINGS.

The Comptroller General shall conduct a study on the impact of State laws regulating securities offerings, or "Blue Sky laws", on offerings made under Regulation A (17 CFR 230.251 et seq.).

Requires that the Comptroller General do a study on the impact of state laws on offerings made under the federal Regulation A.

The Comptroller General shall transmit a report on the findings of the study to the Committee on Financial Services of the House of Representatives, and the Committee on Banking, Housing, and Urban Affairs of the Senate not later than 3 months after the date of enactment of this Act.

Analysis

This section of the act creates another way small companies can use the capital markets to raise capital. It establishes that the SEC must increase the amount of capital companies can raise using what are known as Regulation A exemptions to $50 million. Historically, Regulation A offerings have been much lower than Regulation D[1] offerings.[2] This section of the JOBS Act seeks to change that.

One of the reasons this is important is that, after years of denial, lawmakers have begun to recognize not only that capital is an issue, but also that the issue is so serious that it requires an "all of the above" approach. The law's new "on-ramps," increases in old and outdated regulatory capital limits, and efforts to make use of the Internet and social media start here.

---

[1] Regulation D comprises a series of exemptions that allow companies to sell equity to private, accredited investors.

[2] See Rutheford B. Campbell, Jr., Regulation A: Small Business' Search for a Moderate Capital, University of Kentucky College of Law, *Delaware Journal of Corporate Law*, vol. 31, no. 1, pp. 77–123, 2005.

11

Title V

Private Company Flexibility and Growth

If a company has fewer than 750 shareholders and less than $1 million in assets, long established rules exempt that firm from having to register its securities with the SEC. The JOBS Act revamps these limits to $10 million in assets and either of the following:

- 2,000 shareholders or

- 500 nonaccredited investors.

The JOBS Act specifies how the 2,000-person limit is to be calculated. Included in the calculation are persons who received the stock as part of an employee compensation arrangement.

The relaxation of this limit should facilitate the creation and use of online capital-raising tools targeted to accredited investors.

SEC. 501. THRESHOLD FOR REGISTRATION.

Section 12(g)(1)(A) of the Securities Exchange Act of 1934 (15 U.S.C. 78l(g)(1)(A)) is amended to read as follows:

"(A) within 120 days after the last day of its first fiscal year ended on which the issuer has total assets exceeding $10,000,000 and a class of equity security (other than an exempted security) held of record by either—

Requires the SEC to exempt from registration companies that have less than $10 million in assets and equity securities held by fewer than 2,000 persons or 500 nonaccredited investors.

"(i) 2,000 persons, or

"(ii) 500 persons who are not accredited investors (as such term is defined by the Commission), and".

SEC. 502. EMPLOYEES.

Section 12(g)(5) of the Securities Exchange Act of 1934 (15 U.S.C. 78l(g)(5)), as amended by section 302, is amended in subparagraph (A) by adding at the end the following: "For purposes of determining whether an issuer is required to register a security with the Commission pursuant to paragraph (1), the definition of 'held of record' shall not include securities held by persons who received the securities pursuant to an employee compensation plan in transactions exempted from the registration requirements of section 5 of the Securities Act of 1933."

SEC. 503. COMMISSION RULEMAKING.

The Securities and Exchange Commission shall revise the definition of "held of record" pursuant to section 12(g)(5) of the Securities Exchange Act of 1934 (15 U.S.C. 78l(g)(5)) to implement the amendment made by section 502. The Commission shall also adopt safe harbor provisions that issuers can follow when determining whether holders of their securities received the securities pursuant to an employee compensation plan in transactions that were exempt from the registration requirements of section 5 of the Securities Act of 1933.

SEC. 504. COMMISSION STUDY OF ENFORCEMENT AUTHORITY UNDER RULE 12G5–1.

The Securities and Exchange Commission shall examine its authority to enforce Rule 12g5–1 to determine if new enforcement tools are needed to enforce the anti-evasion provision contained in subsection (b)(3) of the rule, and shall, not later than 120 days after the date of enactment of this Act transmit its recommendations to Congress.

Summary

Title V relaxes shareholder limits that trigger exactly when a company must begin registering and reporting security sales offerings to the SEC. There is considerable debate about the impact this section of the JOBS Act will have. Some companies, including Google, have claimed that the shareholder reporting limits forced them to go public before they would have otherwise. Others have claimed that "fewer than 12 companies" will benefit from this rule change.[1]

---

[1] Telis Demos, "Fewer than 12 Companies to Benefit from Rule Change," *Financial Times*, June 24, 2011.

It seems reasonable to assume that the higher the number of shareholders you can have before you must report to the SEC and start following all the disclosure rules, the longer you will take to do so. Given the elevated number of shareholders one observes in a crowdfunding solicitation, we think, unless the trigger point was raised to, say, 100,000 shareholders, that the impact of this provision on capital raising activity will be helpful, but minimal.

Title VI
Capital Expansion

Title VI of the JOBS Act focuses on banks, and does for them what Title V did for other companies. It says banks don't need to register with the SEC until they have $10 million in assets and a certain number of shareholders. It also expands the number of those shareholders for these institutions from 500 to 2,000 before triggering the registration requirement, with no qualification concerning accredited vs. nonaccredited persons.

SEC. 601. SHAREHOLDER THRESHOLD FOR REGISTRATION.

(a) AMENDMENTS TO SECTION 12 OF THE SECURITIES EXCHANGE ACT OF 1934.—Section 12(g) of the Securities Exchange Act of 1934 (15 U.S.C. 78l(g)) is further amended—

(1) in paragraph (1), by amending subparagraph (B) to read as follows:

"(B) in the case of an issuer that is a bank or a bank holding company, as such term is defined in section 2 of the Bank Holding Company Act of 1956 (12 U.S.C. 1841), not later than 120 days after the last day of its first fiscal year ended after the effective date of this subsection, on which the issuer has total assets exceeding $10,000,000 and a class of equity security (other than an exempted security) held of record by 2,000 or more persons,"; and

Requires the SEC to increase the registration starting point from $1 million to $10 million. Raises the number of shareholders a bank can have before registration is required from 500 to 2,000 persons.

(2) in paragraph (4), by striking "three hundred" and inserting "300 persons, or, in the case of a bank or a bank holding company, as such term is defined in section 2 of the Bank Holding Company Act of 1956 (12 U.S.C. 1841), 1,200 persons".

(b) AMENDMENTS TO SECTION 15 OF THE SECURITIES EXCHANGE ACT OF 1934.—Section 15(d) of the Securities Exchange Act of 1934 (15 U.S.C. 78o(d)) is amended, in the third sentence, by striking "three hundred" and inserting "300 persons, or, in the case of bank or a bank holding company, as such term is defined in section 2 of the Bank Holding Company Act of 1956 (12 U.S.C. 1841), 1,200 persons".

> *Requires the SEC to terminate registration if the number of persons holding shares on record declines below 1,200.*

SEC. 602. RULEMAKING.

Not later than 1 year after the date of enactment of this Act, the Securities and Exchange Commission shall issue final regulations to implement this title and the amendments made by this title.

> *Requires the SEC to issue rules to implement this part of the act.*

Analysis

This section of the JOBS Act seeks to reduce disclosure and registration requirements affecting banks and thrift institutions. Most small businesses will not be affected. To the extent that banks and thrifts use their newfound regulatory freedom and the money resulting from it (generated by an increase in demand from small businesses and a reduction in costs) to make small business loans, then small businesses in areas served by these banks will be better off. Some small banks will increase lending, other things equal, but most will probably capture the cost savings and pay them out to shareholders or management.

Banks and thrifts that deregister based on fewer than 1,200 shareholders—in other words, choose not to supply current periodic financial and operational information to the SEC—will be marginally less transparent. This may mean a higher degree of investor risk. These institutions will still file periodic financial reports with banking regulatory agencies, however.

For many banks, leaving the capital markets is not an option. These banks and thrifts depend upon institutional investors, and these investors mandate that the bank or thrift register its securities with the SEC as a condition of investing.

Combined with other sections of the JOBS Act, banks may have more access to capital. Time will tell if they use this potential increase in capital access to increase lending activity. More likely, some will and some won't. The general hope is that the combination of new capital access approaches will work symbiotically to significantly increase capital access for small firms.

Title VII

Outreach on Changes to the Law

This title of the JOBS Act follows a pattern established by Section 342 of the Dodd-Frank Wall Street Reform and Consumer Protection Act, which requires the creation of an Office of Minority and Women Inclusion at 29 federal agencies to "monitor the diversity efforts of the agencies, the regulated entities and agency contractors."

As we saw in the recent economic collapse, financial institutions were adept at promoting themselves as socially responsible in devising products to help minority communities—products such as subprime mortgages that turned out to hurt more than help them. This part of the law is designed to make sure that a multiplicity of businesses have access to crowdfunding, or are, at the very least, aware it exists.[1]

SEC. 701. OUTREACH BY THE COMMISSION.

The Securities and Exchange Commission shall provide online information and conduct outreach to inform small and medium sized businesses, women owned businesses, veteran owned businesses, and minority owned businesses of the changes made by this Act.

Analysis

One of the most overlooked but important provisions of Dodd-Frank requires federal banking agencies to examine diversity efforts at the 27,000 financial institutions the 29 federal agencies regulate. While the success or failure of

---

[1] William Michael Cunningham, "Crowdfunding and Women and Minority Firms," *The Washington Post*, June 3, 2012. Available at: www.washingtonpost.com/business/capitalbusiness/commentary-crowdfunding-can-provide-new-financing-option-for-minority-firms/2012/06/01/gJQAThq7BV_story.html.

this effort rests on the level of scrutiny the agencies will apply to the financial institutions and the techniques they use, knowing that they are being watched will spur the financial institutions to hire more minority employees and spend more money with minority contractors.[2] This should be good for women and minority firms seeking to crowdfund. Those that are successful in attracting business from government agencies on the lookout for competent women- and minority-owned firms that can provide value-adding services and goods on a competitive basis should be able to obtain financing on better terms via crowdfunding.

According to the Census Bureau, between 2002 and 2007, the number of minority-owned firms jumped by 45.6%—twice the overall rate of U.S. businesses.

Still, they lag those owned by nonminorities in just about every category. While minorities in 2010 comprised 35% of the nation's population, they represented 15% of business owners, according to American Express Open.

Minority-owned firms in general, according to the Small Business Administration (SBA), generate less revenue than their nonminority counterparts. For instance, black-owned businesses earn 43 cents for every dollar earned by white-owned firms, according to the SBA.

Moreover, a study conducted by the Commerce Department concluded that women- and minority-owned firms "experience higher loan denial probabilities and pay higher interest rates than white-owned businesses even after controlling for differences in credit-worthiness, and other factors."[3] The failure rate of minority businesses is higher than that of nonminority firms, according to the Commerce Department's Minority Business Development Agency, partly because of lack of capital.

Table 13-1 lists Office of Minority and Women Inclusion (OMWI) offices and the administrator of each. For minority- and women-owned companies looking to grow via crowdfunding, if you sell (or could potentially sell) goods and services to the federal government, this table provides the names of persons you may wish to contact.

---

[2] Cunningham, "Dodd Frank 342 and Minority Firms," *The Washington Post,* June 5, 2011. Available at: www.washingtonpost.com/business/capitalbusiness/commentary-new-law-a-boon-for-women--and-minority-owned-firms/2011/06/01/AGxHCfJH_story.html.

[3] Robert W. Fairlie and Alicia M. Robb, *Disparities in Capital Access between Minority and Non-Minority-Owned Businesses: The Troubling Reality of Capital Limitations Faced by MBEs,* U.S. Department of Commerce, Minority Business Development Agency, January 2010: 21.

Table 13-1. OMWI Offices and Administrators

Agency	Person Responsible for OMWI Office
Treasury – Domestic Finance	Lorraine Cole
Treasury – Economic Policy	Lorraine Cole
Treasury – General Counsel	Lorraine Cole
Treasury – International Affairs	Lorraine Cole
Treasury – Legislative Affairs	Lorraine Cole
Treasury – Management/CFO	Lorraine Cole
Treasury – Public Affairs	Lorraine Cole
Treasury – Tax Policy	Lorraine Cole
Treasury – Terrorism and Financial Intelligence (TFI)	Lorraine Cole
Treasury – Treasurer of the United States	Lorraine Cole
Federal Deposit Insurance Corporation	D. Michael Collins
Federal Housing Finance Agency	Lee Bowman
Federal Reserve Bank of Boston	Marques Benton
Federal Reserve Bank of New York	Diane Ashley
Federal Reserve Bank of Philadelphia	Mary Ann Hood
Federal Reserve Bank of Cleveland	Peggy Velimesis
Federal Reserve Bank of Chicago	Valerie Van Meter
Federal Reserve Bank of St. Louis	James Price
Federal Reserve Bank of Minneapolis	Duane Carter
Federal Reserve Bank of Kansas City	Donna Ward
Federal Reserve Bank of Dallas	Tyrone Gholson
Federal Reserve Bank of San Francisco	Susan Sutherland
Federal Reserve Bank of Richmond	Tammy Cummings

Agency	Person Responsible for OMWI Office
Federal Reserve Bank of Atlanta	Joan Buchanan
Board of Governors of the Federal Reserve System	Shelia Clark
National Credit Union Administration	Tawana James
Office of the Comptroller of the Currency	Joyce Cofield
Securities and Exchange Commission	Juanita Cole
Consumer Financial Protection Bureau	Stuart Ishimaru

Table 13-2 provides information on minority business contracting activities and shows the dollar amount each of these agencies spent with women and minority firms. These spending figures are reported by each of the agencies with an Office of Women and Minority Inclusion (OMWI). Table 13.2 excludes U.S. Treasury department offices.

These data give some indication of the amount of money available to support crowdfunding efforts by veteran-, women-, and minority-owned firms with federal contracts. After all, companies with federal contracts in place are far less risky than startups. OMWI offices reported spending $2.8 billion with these firms. Veteran-, women-, and minority-owned firms with federal contracts may be some of the safest firms to support via crowdfunding.

To help you visualize the data in Table 13-2, Figure 13-1 and 13-2 shows spending by these agencies. The figures show data for 2011, by agency. Figure 13-1 shows spending by Federal Reserve Banks and offices. Dollars spent are shown by the line and are measured on the left side axis. The percentage of all spending that these contracts represent by an agency is shown by the bars and is measured on the right side axis.

Table 13-2. OMWI Agency Spending, in Dollars, 2011

	Total	Minority	Woman	Minority & Women Total	% Minority	% Women
FRB StL	$ 44,170,000	$ 477,000	$ 2,654,600	$ 3,131,600	1.080%	6.010%
FRBPhilly	$ 43,220,000	$ 1,910,000	$ 2,930,000	$ 4,840,000	4.419%	6.779%
FRBRich	$ 257,230,000	$ 3,000,000	$ 5,070,000	$ 8,070,000	1.166%	1.971%
FRBDallas	$ 62,570,000	$ 1,514,194	$ 1,989,726	$ 3,503,920	2.420%	3.180%
FRBMpls	$ 31,700,000	$ 5,900,000	$ 1,600,000	$ 7,500,000	18.612%	5.047%
FRN NY	$ 190,846,795	$ 2,843,165	$ 2,838,524	$ 5,681,689	1.490%	1.487%
FRB Clev	$ 27,433,027	$ 663,568	$ 2,374,188	$ 3,037,756	2.419%	8.654%
FRB Chi	$ 51,584,470	$ 2,750,000	$ 1,570,000	$ 4,320,000	5.331%	3.044%
FRB Atl	$ 62,340,000	$ 1,070,000	$ 2,060,000	$ 3,130,000	1.716%	3.304%
FRB BoG	$ 125,070,569	$ 9,028,526	$ 4,237,038	$ 15,414,147	7.219%	3.388%
FRBSF	$ 55,500,000	$ 1,594,400	$ 1,591,751	$ 3,190,000	2.873%	2.868%
FRBKC	$ 37,500,000	$ 618,000	$ 4,000,000	$ 4,600,000	1.648%	10.667%

	Total	Minority	Woman	Minority & Women Total	% Minority	% Women
FRBBos	$ 33,270,000	$ 570,000	$ 960,000	$ 1,530,000	1.713%	2.885%
FHFA	$ 69,914,642	$ 16,954,301	$ 2,307,183	$ 19,261,483	24.250%	3.300%
SEC	$ 228,000,000	$ 38,380,000	$ 15,690,000	$ 54,070,000	16.833%	6.882%
FDIC	$ 1,441,600,000	$ 313,400,000	$ 155,300,000	$ 416,500,000	21.740%	10.773%
NCUA	$ 49,600,000	Not reported	Not reported	$ 6,800,000		
Total	$ 211,549,503	$ 400,673,154	$ 207,173,010	$ 564,580,595		
Avg	$ 165,385,265	$ 5,818,210	$ 3,458,201	$ 33,210,623		
Median	$ 55,500,000	$ 1,910,000	$ 2,374,188	$ 4,840,000		

Source: Data compiled by the author from 2011 Annual OMWI Office Reports issued by each agency listed above.

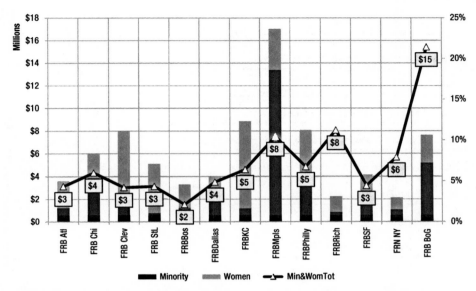

Figure 13-1. Dollars and percentages of contracts to minority- and women-owned firms by Federal Reserve Banks and Board of Governors, 2011.

Table 13-3 gives the full agency names.

Table 13-3. Full Bank and Agency Names

FRB StL= Federal Reserve Bank of St. Louis
FRBPhilly = Federal Reserve Bank of Philadelphia
FRBRich = Federal Reserve Bank of Richmond
FRBDallas = Federal Reserve Bank of Dallas
FRBMpls = Federal Reserve Bank of Minneapolis
FRN NY = Federal Reserve Bank of New York
FRB Clev = Federal Reserve Bank of Cleveland
FRB Chi = Federal Reserve Bank of Chicago
FRB Atl = Federal Reserve Bank of Atlanta
FRB BoG = Federal Reserve Board of Governors
FRBSF = Federal Reserve Bank of San Francisco

FRBKC = Federal Reserve Bank of Kansas City
FRBBos = Federal Reserve Bank of Boston
FHFA = Federal Housing Finance Agency
SEC = Securities and Exchange Commission
FDIC = Federal Deposit Insurance Corporation
NCUA = National Credit Union Administration
Total = Total Dollars Spent
Avg = Average
Median = Median

Figure 13-2 shows the same data as in Figure 13-1 for the Federal Housing Finance Agency (FHFA), the Securities and Exchange Commission (SEC), and the Federal Deposit Insurance Corporation (FDIC).

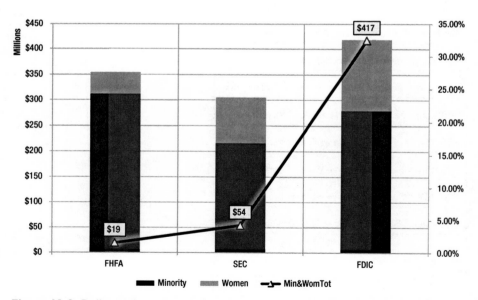

Figure 13-2. Dollars and percentage of total contracts to minority and women-owned firms, by FHFA, SEC, and FDIC.

As the figures and tables show, the federal government spends significant amounts of money with women and minority firms. If your firm meets this definition (51% or more of the common stock owned by women or minorities), you may wish to consider trying to do business with one or more of the agencies listed there.

Crowdfunding and Status as a Minority- or Women-owned company

As we have seen, crowdfunding can mean that hundreds of people invest in your firm or project. A natural question concerns whether or not having hundreds, possibly thousands, of investors will change a firm's status as women- or minority-owned. After all, unless you can verify the race and gender of the persons investing, you cannot be sure to meet the definition above.

We do not believe this should be a concern. As long as you offer less than the majority of the shares in your firm, and as long as the persons who own at least 51% of the equity in your firm are minorities or women, then your firm will continue to have the status of a minority- or women-owned firm. Might this be an issue for subsequent offering, should you decide to sell more stock? Yes, but I believe you should cross that bridge when (and if) you get to it.

Appendix

The JOBS Act is a significant revision to the rules regarding access to capital for startup, small, and medium-sized companies. This appendix provides commentary and partial text of laws related to the JOBS Act to give you added context. I want to make sure you have a comprehensive set of information, including the full text of all relevant securities laws.

In addition, I have included a sample "Pitch" deck, as described in Chapter 5. This presentation can be used to help you solicit capital online.

Securities Act of 1933

The SEC Act of 1933 mandates that any financial security sale be registered with the Securities and Exchange Commission (SEC) if that sale requires or uses the tools and facilities of interstate commerce (telephone, telegraph, and now, the Internet). In this sense, the JOBS Act adds the Internet to the list of interstate commerce tools covered by the SEC. The 1933 Act focuses on disclosure. In other words, it mandates that security sellers honestly and completely reveal all relevant information to security buyers.

Even with the debut of the JOBS Act, the requirements of the 1933 Act are still in force. It is the law that governs most financial security and investment disclosure rules and requirements. Here it is in full:

[As Amended through P.L. 112-106, approved April 5, 2012]

www.sec.gov/about/laws/sa33.pdf

Securities Exchange Act of 1934

The Securities Exchange Act of 1934 covers what happens after securities are created under the 1933 Act. It covers "secondary trading" of investment securities, typically bonds and stocks. Given this, the 1934 Act covers the trading of securities created and issued under the JOBS Act. The act also covers security exchanges, like the New York Stock Exchange. Given that crowdfunding portals may begin to act, as some point, as trading facilities for crowdfunded securities, the relevance of the 1934 Act is clear. Here is the law:

[As Amended through P.L. 112-106, approved April 5, 2012]

www.sec.gov/about/laws/sea34.pdf

Dodd-Frank, Section 342

Section 342 of the Dodd-Frank Wall Street Reform and Consumer Protection Act establishes Offices of Women and Minority Inclusion at twenty-nine financial institution regulatory agencies. I include this section here because of the linkage between it and Title VII of the JOBS Act, which mandates that the SEC reach out to businesses owned by women, members of minority groups, and veterans to make sure they are fully informed about the business capital and startup funding opportunities the JOBS Act provides. As I note in other sections of the book, it is my belief that smart women, minority, and veteran businesspeople will see the linkage and use the Act to obtain capital for businesses that provide services to one or more of the 29 offices covered by Section 342.

SEC. 342. OFFICE OF MINORITY AND WOMEN INCLUSION.

(a) OFFICE OF MINORITY AND WOMEN INCLUSION.—

(1) ESTABLISHMENT.—

(A) IN GENERAL.—Except as provided in subparagraph (B), not later than 6 months after the date of enactment of this Act, each agency shall establish an Office of Minority and Women Inclusion that shall be responsible for all matters of the agency relating to diversity in management, employment, and business activities.

(B) BUREAU.—The Bureau shall establish an Office of Minority and Women Inclusion not later than 6 months after the designated transfer date established under section 1062.

(1) IN GENERAL.—The Director of each Office shall be appointed by, and shall report to, the agency administrator. The position of Director shall be a career reserved position in the Senior Executive Service, as that position is defined in section 3132 of title 5, United States Code, or an equivalent designation.

(2) DUTIES.—Each Director shall develop standards for—

(A) equal employment opportunity and the racial, ethnic, and gender diversity of the workforce and senior management of the agency;

(B) increased participation of minority-owned and women-owned businesses in the programs and contracts of the agency, including standards for coordinating technical assistance to such businesses; and

(C) assessing the diversity policies and practices of entities regulated by the agency.

(3) OTHER DUTIES.—Each Director shall advise the agency administrator on the impact of the policies and regulations of the agency on minority-owned and women-owned businesses.

PUBLIC LAW 107–204—JULY 30, 2002: Sarbanes-Oxley

The Sarbanes-Oxley Act of 2002 (SOX) attempted to correct flaws in the relationship between investment analysts, investment banks and companies issuing stock. While the recent financial crisis has raised grave questions about just how successful SOX was, the law still provides the current set of rules governing securities analysts. Given changes in the JOBS Act directed to these analysts, allowing them to issue reports about crowdfunded companies, I thought it important to include the original statute related to analysts so that you would be fully informed about current law in this area.

SEC. 501. TREATMENT OF SECURITIES ANALYSTS BY REGISTERED SECURITIES ASSOCIATIONS AND NATIONAL SECURITIES EXCHANGES.

(a) RULES REGARDING SECURITIES ANALYSTS.—The Securities Exchange Act of 1934 (15 U.S.C. 78a et seq.) is amended by inserting after section 15C the following new section:

"SEC. 15D. SECURITIES ANALYSTS AND RESEARCH REPORTS.

"(a) ANALYST PROTECTIONS.—The Commission, or upon the authorization and direction of the Commission, a registered securities association or national securities exchange, shall have adopted, not later than 1 year after the date of enactment of this section, rules reasonably designed to address conflicts of interest that can arise when securities analysts recommend equity securities in research reports and public appearances, in order to improve the objectivity of research and provide investors with more useful and reliable information, including rules designed—

"(1) to foster greater public confidence in securities research, and to protect the objectivity and independence of securities analysts, by—

"(A) restricting the prepublication clearance or approval of research reports by persons employed by the broker or dealer who are engaged in investment banking activities, or persons not directly responsible for investment research, other than legal or compliance staff;

"(B) limiting the supervision and compensatory evaluation of securities analysts to officials employed by the broker or dealer who are not engaged in investment banking activities; and

"(C) requiring that a broker or dealer and persons employed by a broker or dealer who are involved with investment banking activities may not, directly or indirectly, retaliate against or threaten to retaliate against any securities analyst employed by that broker or dealer or its affiliates as a result of an adverse, negative, or otherwise unfavorable research report that may adversely affect the present or prospective investment banking relationship of the broker or dealer with the issuer that is the subject of the research report, except that such rules may not limit the authority of a broker or dealer to discipline a securities analyst for causes other than such research report in accordance with the policies and procedures of the firm;

"(2) to define periods during which brokers or dealers who have participated, or are to participate, in a public offering of securities as underwriters or dealers should not publish or otherwise distribute research reports relating to such securities or to the issuer of such securities;

"(3) to establish structural and institutional safeguards within registered brokers or dealers to assure that securities analysts are separated by appropriate informational partitions within the firm from the review, pressure, or oversight of those whose involvement in investment banking activities might potentially bias their judgment or supervision; and

"(4) to address such other issues as the Commission, or such association or exchange, determines appropriate.

"(b) DISCLOSURE.— The Commission, or upon the authorization and direction of the Commission, a registered securities association or national securities exchange, shall have adopted, not later than 1 year after the date of enactment of this section, rules reasonably designed to require each securities analyst to disclose in public appearances, and each registered broker or dealer to disclose in each research report, as applicable, conflicts of interest that are known or should have been known by the securities analyst or the broker or dealer, to exist at the time of the appearance or the date of distribution of the report, including—

"(1) the extent to which the securities analyst has debt or equity investments in the issuer that is the subject of the appearance or research report;

"(2) whether any compensation has been received by the registered broker or dealer, or any affiliate thereof, including the securities analyst, from the issuer that is the subject of the appearance or research report, subject to such exemptions as the Commission may determine appropriate and necessary to prevent disclosure by virtue of this paragraph of material non-public information regarding specific potential future investment banking transactions of such issuer, as is appropriate in the public interest and consistent with the protection of investors;

"(3) whether an issuer, the securities of which are recommended in the appearance or research report, currently is, or during the 1-year period preceding the date of the appearance or date of distribution of the report has been, a client of the registered broker or dealer, and if so, stating the types of services provided to the issuer;

"(4) whether the securities analyst received compensation with respect to a research report, based upon (among any other factors) the investment banking revenues (either generally or specifically earned from the issuer being analyzed) of the registered broker or dealer; and

"(5) such other disclosures of conflicts of interest that are material to investors, research analysts, or the broker or dealer as the Commission, or such association or exchange, determines appropriate.

"(c) DEFINITIONS.—In this section—

"(1) the term 'securities analyst' means any associated person of a registered broker or dealer that is principally responsible for, and any associated person who reports directly or indirectly to a securities analyst in connection with, the preparation of the substance of a research report, whether or not any such person has the job title of 'securities analyst';

and

"(2) the term 'research report' means a written or electronic communication that includes an analysis of equity securities of individual companies or industries, and that provides information reasonably sufficient upon which to base an investment decision."

(b) ENFORCEMENT.—Section 21B(a) of the Securities Exchange Act of 1934 (15 U.S.C. 78u–2(a)) is amended by inserting "15D," before "15B."

(c) COMMISSION AUTHORITY.— The Commission may promulgate and amend its regulations, or direct a registered securities association or national securities exchange to promulgate and amend its rules, to carry out section 15D of the Securities Exchange Act of 1934, as added by this section, as is necessary for the protection of investors and in the public interest.

From: The Sarbanes-Oxley Act of 2002. Available at: www.sec.gov/about/laws/soa2002.pdf

PUBLIC LAW 111 – 203: DODD-FRANK WALL STREET REFORM AND CONSUMER PROTECTION ACT

Other sections of Dodd-Frank are relevant for those seeking to fully understand the JOBS Act. One of the Dodd-Frank sections concerns executive compensation and disclosures. Crowdfunded companies are now exempt from some of these requirements. I have included the section below so that you can understand what, exactly, is being exempted.

SEC. 951. SHAREHOLDER VOTE ON EXECUTIVE COMPENSATION DISCLOSURES.

The Securities Exchange Act of 1934 (15 U.S.C. 78a et seq.) is amended by inserting after section 14 (15 U.S.C. 78n) the following:

"SEC. 14A. SHAREHOLDER APPROVAL OF EXECUTIVE COMPENSATION.

"(a) SEPARATE RESOLUTION REQUIRED.—

"(1) IN GENERAL.—Not less frequently than once every 3 years, a proxy or consent or authorization for an annual or other meeting of the shareholders for which the proxy solicitation rules of the Commission require compensation disclosure shall include a separate resolution subject to shareholder vote to approve the compensation of executives, as disclosed pursuant to section 229.402 of title 17, Code of Federal Regulations, or any successor thereto.

"(2) FREQUENCY OF VOTE.—Not less frequently than once every 6 years, a proxy or consent or authorization for an annual or other meeting of the shareholders for which the proxy solicitation rules of the Commission require compensation disclosure shall include a separate resolution subject to shareholder vote to determine whether votes on the resolutions required under paragraph (1) will occur every 1, 2, or 3 years.

"(3) EFFECTIVE DATE.—The proxy or consent or authorization for the first annual or other meeting of the shareholders occurring after the end of the 6-month period beginning on the date of enactment of this section shall include—

"(A) the resolution described in paragraph (1); and

"(B) a separate resolution subject to shareholder vote to determine whether votes on the resolutions required under paragraph (1) will occur every 1, 2, or 3 years.

"(b) SHAREHOLDER APPROVAL OF GOLDEN PARACHUTE COMPEN-SATION.—

"(1) DISCLOSURE.—In any proxy or consent solicitation material (the solicitation of which is subject to the rules of the Commission pursuant to subsection (a)) for a meeting of the shareholders occurring after the end of the 6-month period beginning on the date of enactment of this section, at which shareholders are asked to approve an acquisition, merger, consolidation, or proposed sale or other disposition of all or substantially all the assets of an issuer, the person making such solicitation shall disclose in the proxy or consent solicitation material, in a clear and simple form in accordance with regulations to be promulgated by the Commission, any agreements or understandings that such person has with any named executive officers of such issuer (or of the acquiring issuer, if such issuer is not the acquiring issuer) concerning any type of compensation (whether present, deferred, or contingent) that is based on or otherwise relates to the acquisition, merger, consolidation, sale, or other disposition of all or substantially all of the assets of the issuer and the aggregate total of all such compensation that may (and the conditions upon which it may) be paid or become payable to or on behalf of such executive officer.

"(2) SHAREHOLDER APPROVAL.—Any proxy or consent or authorization relating to the proxy or consent solicitation material containing the disclosure required by paragraph (1) shall include a separate resolution subject to shareholder vote to approve such agreements or understandings and compensation as disclosed, unless such agreements or understandings have been subject to a shareholder vote under subsection (a).

"(c) RULE OF CONSTRUCTION.—The shareholder vote referred to in subsections (a) and (b) shall not be binding on the issuer or the board of directors of an issuer, and may not be construed—

"(1) as overruling a decision by such issuer or board of directors;

"(2) to create or imply any change to the fiduciary duties of such issuer or board of directors;

"(3) to create or imply any additional fiduciary duties for such issuer or board of directors; or

"(4) to restrict or limit the ability of shareholders to make proposals for inclusion in proxy materials related to executive compensation.

"(d) DISCLOSURE OF VOTES.—Every institutional investment manager subject to section 13(f) shall report at least annually how it voted on any shareholder vote pursuant to subsections (a) and (b), unless such vote is otherwise required to be reported publicly by rule or regulation of the Commission.

"(e) EXEMPTION.—The Commission may, by rule or order, exempt an issuer or class of issuers from the requirement under subsection (a) or (b). In determining whether to make an exemption under this subsection, the Commission shall take into account, among other considerations, whether the requirements under subsections (a) and (b) disproportionately burdens small issuers."

From: The Dodd-Frank Wall Street Reform and Consumer Protection Act.

Available at: www.sec.gov/about/laws/wallstreetreform-cpa.pdf

Sarbanes-Oxley:

SEC. 404. MANAGEMENT ASSESSMENT OF INTERNAL CONTROLS.

As with the executive compensation exemptions that are part of the JOBS Act, crowdfunded companies are exempt from certain disclosure requirements. I have included the section below so that you can understand what, exactly, is being exempted.

(a) RULES REQUIRED.—The Commission shall prescribe rules requiring each annual report required by section 13(a) or 15(d) of the Securities Exchange Act of 1934 (15 U.S.C. 78m or 78o(d)) to contain an internal control report, which shall—

(1) state the responsibility of management for establishing and maintaining an adequate internal control structure and procedures for financial reporting; and

(2) contain an assessment, as of the end of the most recent fiscal year of the issuer, of the effectiveness of the internal control structure and procedures of the issuer for financial reporting.

(b) INTERNAL CONTROL EVALUATION AND REPORTING.—With respect to the internal control assessment required by subsection (a), each registered public accounting firm that prepares or issues the audit report for the issuer shall attest to, and report on, the assessment made by the management of the issuer. An attestation made under this subsection shall be made in accordance with standards for attestation engagements issued or adopted by the Board.

Any such attestation shall not be the subject of a separate engagement.

From: The Sarbanes-Oxley Act of 2002.

Available at: http://www.sec.gov/about/laws/soa2002.pdf

Regulation D

The JOBS Act makes significant changes to what are known as Regulation D security offerings. Capital amounts that can be raised using this exemption have been significantly increased. If you are considering raising capital using Regulation D, you will want to understand what the exact nature of the rules governing it are. Hence, the text below lays out the original text of the regulation governing the exemption.

Regulation D—Rules Governing the Limited Offer and Sale of Securities Without Registration Under the Securities Act of 1933

Source: Sections 230.501 through 230.506 appear at 47 FR 11262, Mar. 16, 1982, unless otherwise noted.

§ 230.500 Use of Regulation D.

Users of Regulation D (§§230.500 et seq.) should note the following:

(a) Regulation D relates to transactions exempted from the registration requirements of section 5 of the Securities Act of 1933 (the Act) (15 U.S.C.77a et seq., as amended). Such transactions are not exempt from the antifraud, civil liability, or other provisions of the federal securities laws. Issuers are reminded of their obligation to provide such further material information, if any, as may be necessary to make the information required under Regulation D, in light of the circumstances under which it is furnished, not misleading.

(b) Nothing in Regulation D obviates the need to comply with any applicable state law relating to the offer and sale of securities. Regulation D is intended to be a basic element in a uniform system of federal-state limited offering exemptions consistent with the provisions of sections 18 and 19(c) of the Act (15 U.S.C. 77r and 77(s)(c)). In those states that have adopted Regulation D, or any version of Regulation D, special attention should be directed to the applicable state laws and regulations, including those relating to registration of persons who receive remuneration in connection with the offer and sale of securities, to disqualification of issuers and other persons associated with offerings based on state administrative orders or judgments, and to requirements for filings of notices of sales.

(c) Attempted compliance with any rule in Regulation D does not act as an exclusive election; the issuer can also claim the availability of any other applicable exemption. For instance, an issuer's failure to satisfy all the terms and conditions of rule 506 (§230.506) shall not raise any presumption that the exemption provided by section 4(2) of the Act (15 U.S.C. 77d(2)) is not available.

(d) Regulation D is available only to the issuer of the securities and not to any affiliate of that issuer or to any other person for resales of the issuer's securities. Regulation D provides an exemption only for the transactions in which the securities are offered or sold by the issuer, not for the securities themselves.

(e) Regulation D may be used for business combinations that involve sales by virtue of rule 145(a) (§230.145(a)) or otherwise.

(f) In view of the objectives of Regulation D and the policies underlying the Act, Regulation D is not available to any issuer for any transaction or chain of transactions that, although in technical compliance with Regulation D, is part of a plan or scheme to evade the registration provisions of the Act. In such cases, registration under the Act is required.

(g) Securities offered and sold outside the United States in accordance with Regulation S (§230.901 through 905) need not be registered under the Act. See Release No. 33–6863. Regulation S may be relied upon for such offers and sales even if coincident offers and sales are made in accordance with Regulation D inside the United States. Thus, for example, persons who are offered and sold securities in accordance with Regulation S would not be counted in the calculation of the number of purchasers under Regulation D. Similarly, proceeds from such sales would not be included in the aggregate offering price. The provisions of this paragraph (g), however, do not apply if the issuer elects to rely solely on Regulation D for offers or sales to persons made outside the United States.

[77 FR 18684, Mar. 28, 2012]

§ 230.501 Definitions and terms used in Regulation D.

As used in Regulation D (§230.500 et seq. of this chapter), the following terms shall have the meaning indicated:

(a) Accredited investor. Accredited investor shall mean any person who comes within any of the following categories, or who the issuer reasonably believes comes within any of the following categories, at the time of the sale of the securities to that person:

(1) Any bank as defined in section 3(a)(2) of the Act, or any savings and loan association or other institution as defined in section 3(a)(5)(A) of the Act whether acting in its individual or fiduciary capacity; any broker or dealer registered pursuant to section 15 of the Securities Exchange Act of 1934; any insurance company as defined in section 2(13) of the Act; any investment company registered under the Investment Company Act of 1940 or a business development company as defined in section 2(a)(48) of that Act; any Small Business Investment Company licensed by the U.S. Small

Business Administration under section 301(c) or (d) of the Small Business Investment Act of 1958; any plan established and maintained by a state, its political subdivisions, or any agency or instrumentality of a state or its political subdivisions, for the benefit of its employees, if such plan has total assets in excess of $5,000,000; any employee benefit plan within the meaning of the Employee Retirement Income Security Act of 1974 if the investment decision is made by a plan fiduciary, as defined in section 3(21) of such act, which is either a bank, savings and loan association, insurance company, or registered investment adviser, or if the employee benefit plan has total assets in excess of $5,000,000 or, if a self-directed plan, with investment decisions made solely by persons that are accredited investors;

(2) Any private business development company as defined in section 202(a)(22) of the Investment Advisers Act of 1940;

(3) Any organization described in section 501(c)(3) of the Internal Revenue Code, corporation, Massachusetts or similar business trust, or partnership, not formed for the specific purpose of acquiring the securities offered, with total assets in excess of $5,000,000;

(4) Any director, executive officer, or general partner of the issuer of the securities being offered or sold, or any director, executive officer, or general partner of a general partner of that issuer;

(5) Any natural person whose individual net worth, or joint net worth with that person's spouse, exceeds $1,000,000.

(i) Except as provided in paragraph (a)(5)(ii) of this section, for purposes of calculating net worth under this paragraph (a)(5):

(A) The person's primary residence shall not be included as an asset;

(B) Indebtedness that is secured by the person's primary residence, up to the estimated fair market value of the primary residence at the time of the sale of securities, shall not be included as a liability (except that if the amount of such indebtedness outstanding at the time of sale of securities exceeds the amount outstanding 60 days before such time, other than as a result of the acquisition of the primary residence, the amount of such excess shall be included as a liability); and

(C) Indebtedness that is secured by the person's primary residence in excess of the estimated fair market value of the primary residence at the time of the sale of securities shall be included as a liability;

(ii) Paragraph (a)(5)(i) of this section will not apply to any calculation of a person's net worth made in connection with a purchase of securities in accordance with a right to purchase such securities, provided that:

(A) Such right was held by the person on July 20, 2010;

(B) The person qualified as an accredited investor on the basis of net worth at the time the person acquired such right; and

(C) The person held securities of the same issuer, other than such right, on July 20, 2010.

(6) Any natural person who had an individual income in excess of $200,000 in each of the two most recent years or joint income with that person's spouse in excess of $300,000 in each of those years and has a reasonable expectation of reaching the same income level in the current year;

(7) Any trust, with total assets in excess of $5,000,000, not formed for the specific purpose of acquiring the securities offered, whose purchase is directed by a sophisticated person as described in §230.506(b)(2)(ii); and

(8) Any entity in which all of the equity owners are accredited investors.

(b) Affiliate. An affiliate of, or person affiliated with, a specified person shall mean a person that directly, or indirectly through one or more intermediaries, controls or is controlled by, or is under common control with, the person specified.

(c) Aggregate offering price. Aggregate offering price shall mean the sum of all cash, services, property, notes, cancellation of debt, or other consideration to be received by an issuer for issuance of its securities. Where securities are being offered for both cash and non-cash consideration, the aggregate offering price shall be based on the price at which the securities are offered for cash. Any portion of the aggregate offering price attributable to cash received in a foreign currency shall be translated into United States currency at the currency exchange rate in effect at a reasonable time prior to or on the date of the sale of the securities. If securities are not offered for cash, the aggregate offering price shall be based on the value of the consideration as established by bona fide sales of that consideration made within a reasonable time, or, in the absence of sales, on the fair value as determined by an accepted standard. Such valuations of non-cash consideration must be reasonable at the time made.

(d) Business combination. Business combination shall mean any transaction of the type specified in paragraph (a) of Rule 145 under the Act (17 CFR 230.145) and any transaction involving the acquisition by one issuer, in exchange for all or a part of its own or its parent's stock, of stock of another issuer if, immediately after the acquisition, the acquiring issuer has control of the other issuer (whether or not it had control before the acquisition).

(e) Calculation of number of purchasers. For purposes of calculating the number of purchasers under §§230.505(b) and 230.506(b) only, the following shall apply:

(1) The following purchasers shall be excluded:

(i) Any relative, spouse or relative of the spouse of a purchaser who has the same primary residence as the purchaser;

(ii) Any trust or estate in which a purchaser and any of the persons related to him as specified in paragraph (e)(1)(i) or (e)(1)(iii) of this section collectively have more than 50 percent of the beneficial interest (excluding contingent interests);

(iii) Any corporation or other organization of which a purchaser and any of the persons related to him as specified in paragraph (e)(1)(i) or (e)(1)(ii) of this section collectively are beneficial owners of more than 50 percent of the equity securities (excluding directors' qualifying shares) or equity interests; and

(iv) Any accredited investor.

(2) A corporation, partnership or other entity shall be counted as one purchaser. If, however, that entity is organized for the specific purpose of acquiring the securities offered and is not an accredited investor under paragraph (a)(8) of this section, then each beneficial owner of equity securities or equity interests in the entity shall count as a separate purchaser for all provisions of Regulation D (§§230.501–230.508), except to the extent provided in paragraph (e)(1) of this section.

(3) A non-contributory employee benefit plan within the meaning of Title I of the Employee Retirement Income Security Act of 1974 shall be counted as one purchaser where the trustee makes all investment decisions for the plan.

Note: The issuer must satisfy all the other provisions of Regulation D for all purchasers whether or not they are included in calculating the number of purchasers. Clients of an investment adviser or customers of a broker or dealer shall be considered the "purchasers" under Regulation D regardless of the amount of discretion given to the investment adviser or broker or dealer to act on behalf of the client or customer.

(f) Executive officer. Executive officer shall mean the president, any vice president in charge of a principal business unit, division or function (such as sales, administration or finance), any other officer who performs a policy making function, or any other person who performs similar policy making functions for the issuer. Executive officers of subsidiaries may be deemed executive officers of the issuer if they perform such policy making functions for the issuer.

(g) Issuer. The definition of the term issuer in section 2(4) of the Act shall apply, except that in the case of a proceeding under the Federal Bankruptcy Code (11 U.S.C. 101 et seq.), the trustee or debtor in possession shall be considered the issuer in an offering under a plan or reorganization, if the securities are to be issued under the plan.

(h) Purchaser representative. Purchaser representative shall mean any person who satisfies all of the following conditions or who the issuer reasonably believes satisfies all of the following conditions:

(1) Is not an affiliate, director, officer or other employee of the issuer, or beneficial owner of 10 percent or more of any class of the equity securities or 10 percent or more of the equity interest in the issuer, except where the purchaser is:

(i) A relative of the purchaser representative by blood, marriage or adoption and not more remote than a first cousin;

(ii) A trust or estate in which the purchaser representative and any persons related to him as specified in paragraph (h)(1)(i) or (h)(1)(iii) of this section collectively have more than 50 percent of the beneficial interest (excluding contingent interest) or of which the purchaser representative serves as trustee, executor, or in any similar capacity; or

(iii) A corporation or other organization of which the purchaser representative and any persons related to him as specified in paragraph (h)(1)(i) or (h)(1)(ii) of this section collectively are the beneficial owners of more than 50 percent of the equity securities (excluding directors' qualifying shares) or equity interests;

(2) Has such knowledge and experience in financial and business matters that he is capable of evaluating, alone, or together with other purchaser representatives of the purchaser, or together with the purchaser, the merits and risks of the prospective investment;

(3) Is acknowledged by the purchaser in writing, during the course of the transaction, to be his purchaser representative in connection with evaluating the merits and risks of the prospective investment; and

(4) Discloses to the purchaser in writing a reasonable time prior to the sale of securities to that purchaser any material relationship between himself or his affiliates and the issuer or its affiliates that then exists, that is mutually understood to be contemplated, or that has existed at any time during the

previous two years, and any compensation received or to be received as a result of such relationship.

Note 1: A person acting as a purchaser representative should consider the applicability of the registration and antifraud provisions relating to brokers and dealers under the Securities Exchange Act of 1934 (Exchange Act) (15 U.S.C. 78a et seq., as amended) and relating to investment advisers under the Investment Advisers Act of 1940.

Note 2: The acknowledgment required by paragraph (h)(3) and the disclosure required by paragraph (h)(4) of this section must be made with specific reference to each prospective investment. Advance blanket acknowledgment, such as for all securities transactions or all private placements, is not sufficient.

Note 3: Disclosure of any material relationships between the purchaser representative or his affiliates and the issuer or its affiliates does not relieve the purchaser representative of his obligation to act in the interest of the purchaser.

[47 FR 11262, Mar. 16, 1982, as amended at 53 FR 7868, Mar. 10, 1988; 54 FR 11372, Mar. 20, 1989; 76 FR 81806, Dec. 29, 2011; 77 FR 18685, Mar. 28, 2012]

§ 230.502 General conditions to be met.

The following conditions shall be applicable to offers and sales made under Regulation D (§230.500 et seq. of this chapter):

(a) Integration. All sales that are part of the same Regulation D offering must meet all of the terms and conditions of Regulation D. Offers and sales that are made more than six months before the start of a Regulation D offering or are made more than six months after completion of a Regulation D offering will not be considered part of that Regulation D offering, so long as during those six month periods there are no offers or sales of securities by or for the issuer that are of the same or a similar class as those offered or sold under Regulation D, other than those offers or sales of securities under an employee benefit plan as defined in rule 405 under the Act (17 CFR 230.405).

Note: The term offering is not defined in the Act or in Regulation D. If the issuer offers or sells securities for which the safe harbor rule in paragraph (a) of this §230.502 is unavailable, the determination as to whether separate sales of securities are part of the same offering (i.e. , are considered integrated) depends on the particular facts and circumstances. Generally, transactions otherwise meeting the requirements of an exemption will not be integrated with simultaneous offerings being made outside the United States in compliance with Regulation S. See Release No. 33–6863.

The following factors should be considered in determining whether offers and sales should be integrated for purposes of the exemptions under Regulation D:

(a) Whether the sales are part of a single plan of financing;

(b) Whether the sales involve issuance of the same class of securities;

(c) Whether the sales have been made at or about the same time;

(d) Whether the same type of consideration is being received; and

(e) Whether the sales are made for the same general purpose.

See Release 33–4552 (November 6, 1962) [27 FR 11316].

(b) Information requirements—(1) When information must be furnished. If the issuer sells securities under §230.505 or §230.506 to any purchaser that is not an accredited investor, the issuer shall furnish the information specified in paragraph (b)(2) of this section to such purchaser a reasonable time prior to sale. The issuer is not required to furnish the specified information to purchasers when it sells securities under §230.504, or to any accredited investor.

Note: When an issuer provides information to investors pursuant to paragraph (b)(1), it should consider providing such information to accredited investors as well, in view of the anti-fraud provisions of the federal securities laws.

(2) Type of information to be furnished.

(i) If the issuer is not subject to the reporting requirements of section 13 or 15(d) of the Exchange Act, at a reasonable time prior to the sale of securities the issuer shall furnish to the purchaser, to the extent material to an understanding of the issuer, its business and the securities being offered:

(A) Non-financial statement information. If the issuer is eligible to use Regulation A (§230.251–263), the same kind of information as would be required in Part II of Form 1–A (§239.90 of this chapter). If the issuer is not eligible to use Regulation A, the same kind of information as required in Part I of a registration statement filed under the Securities Act on the form that the issuer would be entitled to use.

(B) Financial statement information —(1) Offerings up to $2,000,000. The information required in Article 8 of Regulation S–X (§210.8 of this chapter), except that only the issuer's balance sheet, which shall be dated within 120 days of the start of the offering, must be audited.

(2) Offerings up to $7,500,000. The financial statement information required in Form S–1 (§239.10 of this chapter) for smaller reporting companies. If an

issuer, other than a limited partnership, cannot obtain audited financial statements without unreasonable effort or expense, then only the issuer's balance sheet, which shall be dated within 120 days of the start of the offering, must be audited. If the issuer is a limited partnership and cannot obtain the required financial statements without unreasonable effort or expense, it may furnish financial statements that have been prepared on the basis of Federal income tax requirements and examined and reported on in accordance with generally accepted auditing standards by an independent public or certified accountant.

(3) Offerings over $7,500,000. The financial statement as would be required in a registration statement filed under the Act on the form that the issuer would be entitled to use. If an issuer, other than a limited partnership, cannot obtain audited financial statements without unreasonable effort or expense, then only the issuer's balance sheet, which shall be dated within 120 days of the start of the offering, must be audited. If the issuer is a limited partnership and cannot obtain the required financial statements without unreasonable effort or expense, it may furnish financial statements that have been prepared on the basis of Federal income tax requirements and examined and reported on in accordance with generally accepted auditing standards by an independent public or certified accountant.

(C) If the issuer is a foreign private issuer eligible to use Form 20–F (§249.220f of this chapter), the issuer shall disclose the same kind of information required to be included in a registration statement filed under the Act on the form that the issuer would be entitled to use. The financial statements need be certified only to the extent required by paragraph (b)(2)(i) (B) (1), (2) or (3) of this section, as appropriate.

(ii) If the issuer is subject to the reporting requirements of section 13 or 15(d) of the Exchange Act, at a reasonable time prior to the sale of securities the issuer shall furnish to the purchaser the information specified in paragraph (b)(2)(ii)(A) or (B) of this section, and in either event the information specified in paragraph (b)(2)(ii)(C) of this section:

(A) The issuer's annual report to shareholders for the most recent fiscal year, if such annual report meets the requirements of Rules 14a–3 or 14c–3 under the Exchange Act (§240.14a–3 or §240.14c–3 of this chapter), the definitive proxy statement filed in connection with that annual report, and if requested by the purchaser in writing, a copy of the issuer's most recent Form 10–K (§249.310 of this chapter) under the Exchange Act.

(B) The information contained in an annual report on Form 10–K (§249.310 of this chapter) under the Exchange Act or in a registration statement on Form S–1 (§239.11 of this chapter) or S–11 (§239.18 of this chapter) under the

Act or on Form 10 (§249.210 of this chapter) under the Exchange Act, whichever filing is the most recent required to be filed.

(C) The information contained in any reports or documents required to be filed by the issuer under sections 13(a), 14(a), 14(c), and 15(d) of the Exchange Act since the distribution or filing of the report or registration statement specified in paragraphs (b)(2)(ii) (A) or (B), and a brief description of the securities being offered, the use of the proceeds from the offering, and any material changes in the issuer's affairs that are not disclosed in the documents furnished.

(D) If the issuer is a foreign private issuer, the issuer may provide in lieu of the information specified in paragraph (b)(2)(ii) (A) or (B) of this section, the information contained in its most recent filing on Form 20–F or Form F–1 (§239.31 of the chapter).

(iii) Exhibits required to be filed with the Commission as part of a registration statement or report, other than an annual report to shareholders or parts of that report incorporated by reference in a Form 10–K report, need not be furnished to each purchaser that is not an accredited investor if the contents of material exhibits are identified and such exhibits are made available to a purchaser, upon his or her written request, a reasonable time before his or her purchase.

(iv) At a reasonable time prior to the sale of securities to any purchaser that is not an accredited investor in a transaction under §230.505 or §230.506, the issuer shall furnish to the purchaser a brief description in writing of any material written information concerning the offering that has been provided by the issuer to any accredited investor but not previously delivered to such unaccredited purchaser. The issuer shall furnish any portion or all of this information to the purchaser, upon his written request a reasonable time prior to his purchase.

(v) The issuer shall also make available to each purchaser at a reasonable time prior to his purchase of securities in a transaction under §230.505 or §230.506 the opportunity to ask questions and receive answers concerning the terms and conditions of the offering and to obtain any additional information which the issuer possesses or can acquire without unreasonable effort or expense that is necessary to verify the accuracy of information furnished under paragraph (b)(2) (i) or (ii) of this section.

(vi) For business combinations or exchange offers, in addition to information required by Form S–4 (17 CFR 239.25), the issuer shall provide to each purchaser at the time the plan is submitted to security holders, or, with an exchange, during the course of the transaction and prior to sale, written information about any terms or arrangements of the proposed transactions that are materially different from those for all other security holders. For purposes of this subsection, an issuer which is not subject to the reporting requirements of section 13 or 15(d) of the Exchange Act may satisfy the requirements of Part I.B. or C. of Form S–4 by compliance with paragraph (b)(2)(i) of this §230.502.

(vii) At a reasonable time prior to the sale of securities to any purchaser that is not an accredited investor in a transaction under §230.505 or §230.506, the issuer shall advise the purchaser of the limitations on resale in the manner contained in paragraph (d)(2) of this section. Such disclosure may be contained in other materials required to be provided by this paragraph.

(c) Limitation on manner of offering. Except as provided in §230.504(b)(1), neither the issuer nor any person acting on its behalf shall offer or sell the securities by any form of general solicitation or general advertising, including, but not limited to, the following:

(1) Any advertisement, article, notice or other communication published in any newspaper, magazine, or similar media or broadcast over television or radio; and

(2) Any seminar or meeting whose attendees have been invited by any general solicitation or general advertising; Provided, however, that publication by an issuer of a notice in accordance with §230.135c or filing with the Commission by an issuer of a notice of sales on Form D (17 CFR 239.500) in which the issuer has made a good faith and reasonable attempt to comply with the requirements of such form, shall not be deemed to constitute general solicitation or general advertising for purposes of this section; Provided further, that, if the requirements of §230.135e are satisfied, providing any journalist with access to press conferences held outside of the United States, to meetings with issuer or selling security holder representatives conducted outside of the United States, or to written press-related materials released outside the United States, at or in which a present or proposed offering of securities is discussed, will not be deemed to constitute general solicitation or general advertising for purposes of this section.

(d) Limitations on resale. Except as provided in §230.504(b)(1), securities acquired in a transaction under Regulation D shall have the status of securities acquired in a transaction under section 4(2) of the Act and cannot be resold without registration under the Act or an exemption therefrom. The issuer shall exercise reasonable care to assure that the purchasers of the securities are not underwriters within the meaning of section 2(11) of the Act, which reasonable care may be demonstrated by the following:

(1) Reasonable inquiry to determine if the purchaser is acquiring the securities for himself or for other persons;

(2) Written disclosure to each purchaser prior to sale that the securities have not been registered under the Act and, therefore, cannot be resold unless they are registered under the Act or unless an exemption from registration is available; and

(3) Placement of a legend on the certificate or other document that evidences the securities stating that the securities have not been registered under the Act and setting forth or referring to the restrictions on transferability and sale of the securities.

While taking these actions will establish the requisite reasonable care, it is not the exclusive method to demonstrate such care. Other actions by the issuer may satisfy this provision. In addition, §230.502(b)(2)(vii) requires the delivery of written disclosure of the limitations on resale to investors in certain instances.

[47 FR 11262, Mar. 16, 1982, as amended at 47 FR 54771, Dec. 6, 1982; 53 FR 7869, Mar. 11, 1988; 54 FR 11372, Mar. 20, 1989; 55 FR 18322, May 2, 1990; 56 FR 30054, 30055, July 1, 1991; 57 FR 47409, Oct. 16, 1992; 58 FR 26514, May 4, 1993; 59 FR 21650, Apr. 26, 1994; 62 FR 53954, Oct. 17, 1997; 73 FR 969, Jan. 4, 2008; 73 FR 10615, Feb. 27, 2008; 77 FR 18685, Mar. 28, 2012]

§ 230.503 Filing of notice of sales.

(a) When notice of sales on Form D is required and permitted to be filed. (1) An issuer offering or selling securities in reliance on §230.504, §230.505, or §230.506 must file with the Commission a notice of sales containing the information required by Form D (17 CFR 239.500) for each new offering of securities no later than 15 calendar days after the first sale of securities in the offering, unless the end of that period falls on a Saturday, Sunday or holiday, in which case the due date would be the first business day following.

(2) An issuer may file an amendment to a previously filed notice of sales on Form D at any time.

(3) An issuer must file an amendment to a previously filed notice of sales on Form D for an offering:

(i) To correct a material mistake of fact or error in the previously filed notice of sales on Form D, as soon as practicable after discovery of the mistake or error;

(ii) To reflect a change in the information provided in the previously filed notice of sales on Form D, as soon as practicable after the change, except that no amendment is required to reflect a change that occurs after the offering terminates or a change that occurs solely in the following information:

(A) The address or relationship to the issuer of a related person identified in response to Item 3 of the notice of sales on Form D;

(B) An issuer's revenues or aggregate net asset value;

(C) The minimum investment amount, if the change is an increase, or if the change, together with all other changes in that amount since the previously filed notice of sales on Form D, does not result in a decrease of more than 10%;

(D) Any address or state(s) of solicitation shown in response to Item 12 of the notice of sales on Form D;

(E) The total offering amount, if the change is a decrease, or if the change, together with all other changes in that amount since the previously filed notice of sales on Form D, does not result in an increase of more than 10%;

(F) The amount of securities sold in the offering or the amount remaining to be sold;

(G) The number of non-accredited investors who have invested in the offering, as long as the change does not increase the number to more than 35;

(H) The total number of investors who have invested in the offering; or

(I) The amount of sales commissions, finders' fees or use of proceeds for payments to executive officers, directors or promoters, if the change is a decrease, or if the change, together with all other changes in that amount since the previously filed notice of sales on Form D, does not result in an increase of more than 10%; and

(iii) Annually, on or before the first anniversary of the filing of the notice of sales on Form D or the filing of the most recent amendment to the notice of sales on Form D, if the offering is continuing at that time.

(4) An issuer that files an amendment to a previously filed notice of sales on Form D must provide current information in response to all requirements of the notice of sales on Form D regardless of why the amendment is filed.

(b) How notice of sales on Form D must be filed and signed. (1) A notice of sales on Form D must be filed with the Commission in electronic format by means of the Commission's Electronic Data Gathering, Analysis, and Retrieval System (EDGAR) in accordance with EDGAR rules set forth in Regulation S–T (17 CFR Part 232).

(2) Every notice of sales on Form D must be signed by a person duly authorized by the issuer.

[73 FR 10615, Feb. 27, 2008]

§ 230.504 Exemption for limited offerings and sales of securities not exceeding $1,000,000.

(a) Exemption. Offers and sales of securities that satisfy the conditions in paragraph (b) of this §230.504 by an issuer that is not:

(1) Subject to the reporting requirements of section 13 or 15(d) of the Exchange Act,;

(2) An investment company; or

(3) A development stage company that either has no specific business plan or purpose or has indicated that its business plan is to engage in a merger or acquisition with an unidentified company or companies, or other entity or person, shall be exempt from the provision of section 5 of the Act under section 3(b) of the Act.

(b) Conditions to be met —(1) General conditions. To qualify for exemption under this §230.504, offers and sales must satisfy the terms and conditions of §§230.501 and 230.502 (a), (c) and (d), except that the provisions of §230.502 (c) and (d) will not apply to offers and sales of securities under this §230.504 that are made:

(i) Exclusively in one or more states that provide for the registration of the securities, and require the public filing and delivery to investors of a substantive disclosure document before sale, and are made in accordance with those state provisions;

(ii) In one or more states that have no provision for the registration of the securities or the public filing or delivery of a disclosure document before sale, if the securities have been registered in at least one state that provides for such registration, public filing and delivery before sale, offers and sales are made in that state in accordance with such provisions, and the disclosure document is delivered before sale to all purchasers (including those in the states that have no such procedure); or

(iii) Exclusively according to state law exemptions from registration that permit general solicitation and general advertising so long as sales are made only to "accredited investors" as defined in §230.501(a).

(2) The aggregate offering price for an offering of securities under this §230.504, as defined in §230.501(c), shall not exceed $1,000,000, less the aggregate offering price for all securities sold within the twelve months

before the start of and during the offering of securities under this §230.504, in reliance on any exemption under section 3(b), or in violation of section 5(a) of the Securities Act.

Note 1: The calculation of the aggregate offering price is illustrated as follows:

If an issuer sold $900,000 on June 1, 1987 under this §230.504 and an additional $4,100,000 on December 1, 1987 under §230.505, the issuer could not sell any of its securities under this §230.504 until December 1, 1988. Until then the issuer must count the December 1, 1987 sale towards the $1,000,000 limit within the preceding twelve months.

Note 2: If a transaction under §230.504 fails to meet the limitation on the aggregate offering price, it does not affect the availability of this §230.504 for the other transactions considered in applying such limitation. For example, if an issuer sold $1,000,000 worth of its securities on January 1, 1988 under this §230.504 and an additional $500,000 worth on July 1, 1988, this §230.504 would not be available for the later sale, but would still be applicable to the January 1, 1988 sale.

[57 FR 36473, Aug. 13, 1992, as amended at 61 FR 30402, June 14, 1996; 64 FR 11094, Mar. 8, 1999]

§ 230.505 Exemption for limited offers and sales of securities not exceeding $5,000,000.

(a) Exemption. Offers and sales of securities that satisfy the conditions in paragraph (b) of this section by an issuer that is not an investment company shall be exempt from the provisions of section 5 of the Act under section 3(b) of the Act.

(b) Conditions to be met —

(1) General conditions. To qualify for exemption under this section, offers and sales must satisfy the terms and conditions of §§230.501 and 230.502.

(2) Specific conditions —

(i) Limitation on aggregate offering price. The aggregate offering price for an offering of securities under this §230.505, as defined in §203.501(c), shall not exceed $5,000,000, less the aggregate offering price for all securities sold within the twelve months before the start of and during the offering of securities under this section in reliance on any exemption under section 3(b) of the Act or in violation of section 5(a) of the Act.

Note: The calculation of the aggregate offering price is illustrated as follows:

Example 1: If an issuer sold $2,000,000 of its securities on June 1, 1982 under this §230.505 and an additional $1,000,000 on September 1, 1982, the issuer would be permitted to sell only $2,000,000 more under this §230.505 until June 1, 1983. Until that date the issuer must count both prior sales towards the $5,000,000 limit. However, if the issuer made its third sale on June 1, 1983, the issuer could then sell $4,000,000 of its securities because the June 1, 1982 sale would not be within the preceding twelve months.

Example 2: If an issuer sold $500,000 of its securities on June 1, 1982 under §230.504 and an additional $4,500,000 on December 1, 1982 under this section, then the issuer could not sell any of its securities under this section until June 1, 1983. At that time it could sell an additional $500,000 of its securities.

(ii) Limitation on number of purchasers. There are no more than or the issuer reasonably believes that there are no more than 35 purchasers of securities from the issuer in any offering under this section.

(iii) Disqualifications. No exemption under this section shall be available for the securities of any issuer described in §230.262 of Regulation A, except that for purposes of this section only:

(A) The term "filing of the offering statement required by §230.252" as used in §230.262(a), (b) and (c) shall mean the first sale of securities under this section;

(B) The term "underwriter" as used in §230.262 (b) and (c) shall mean a person that has been or will be paid directly or indirectly remuneration for solicitation of purchasers in connection with sales of securities under this section; and

(C) Paragraph (b)(2)(iii) of this section shall not apply to any issuer if the Commission determines, upon a showing of good cause, that it is not necessary under the circumstances that the exemption be denied. Any such determination shall be without prejudice to any other action by the Commission in any other proceeding or matter with respect to the issuer or any other person.

[47 FR 11262, Mar. 16, 1982, as amended at 54 FR 11373, Mar. 20, 1989; 57 FR 36473, Aug. 13, 1992]

§ 230.506 Exemption for limited offers and sales without regard to dollar amount of offering.

(a) Exemption. Offers and sales of securities by an issuer that satisfy the conditions in paragraph (b) of this section shall be deemed to be transactions not involving any public offering within the meaning of section 4(2) of the Act.

(b) Conditions to be met —

(1) General conditions. To qualify for an exemption under this section, offers and sales must satisfy all the terms and conditions of §§230.501 and 230.502.

(2) Specific conditions —

(i) Limitation on number of purchasers. There are no more than or the issuer reasonably believes that there are no more than 35 purchasers of securities from the issuer in any offering under this section.

Note: See §230.501(e) for the calculation of the number of purchasers and §230.502(a) for what may or may not constitute an offering under this section.

(ii) Nature of purchasers. Each purchaser who is not an accredited investor either alone or with his purchaser representative(s) has such knowledge and experience in financial and business matters that he is capable of evaluating the merits and risks of the prospective investment, or the issuer reasonably believes immediately prior to making any sale that such purchaser comes within this description.

[47 FR 11262, Mar. 6, 1982, as amended at 54 FR 11373, Mar. 20, 1989]

§ 230.507 Disqualifying provision relating to exemptions under §§230.504, 230.505 and 230.506.

(a) No exemption under §230.505, §230.505 or §230.506 shall be available for an issuer if such issuer, any of its predecessors or affiliates have been subject to any order, judgment, or decree of any court of competent jurisdiction temporarily, preliminary or permanently enjoining such person for failure to comply with §230.503.

(b) Paragraph (a) of this section shall not apply if the Commission determines, upon a showing of good cause, that it is not necessary under the circumstances that the exemption be denied.

[54 FR 11374, Mar. 20, 1989]

§ 230.508 Insignificant deviations from a term, condition or requirement of Regulation D.

(a) A failure to comply with a term, condition or requirement of §230.504, §230.505 or §230.506 will not result in the loss of the exemption from the requirements of section 5 of the Act for any offer or sale to a particular individual or entity, if the person relying on the exemption shows:

(1) The failure to comply did not pertain to a term, condition or requirement directly intended to protect that particular individual or entity; and

(2) The failure to comply was insignificant with respect to the offering as a whole, provided that any failure to comply with paragraph (c) of §230.502, paragraph (b)(2) of §230.504, paragraphs (b)(2)(i) and (ii) of §230.505 and paragraph (b)(2)(i) of §230.506 shall be deemed to be significant to the offering as a whole; and

(3) A good faith and reasonable attempt was made to comply with all applicable terms, conditions and requirements of §230.504, §230.505 or §230.506.

(b) A transaction made in reliance on §230.504, §230.505 or §230.506 shall comply with all applicable terms, conditions and requirements of Regulation D. Where an exemption is established only through reliance upon paragraph (a) of this section, the failure to comply shall nonetheless be actionable by the Commission under section 20 of the Act.

[54 FR 11374, Mar. 20, 1989, as amended at 57 FR 36473, Aug. 13, 1992]

From: The Electronic Code of Federal regulations. Available at: http://ecfr. gpoaccess.gov/cgi/t/text/text-idx?c=ecfr&sid=944894002777ec9ba2f8951 374bcdb23&rgn=div5&view=text&node=17:2.0.1.1.12&id no=17#17:2.0.1.1.12.0.42

Section 229.301 of Title 17, Code of Federal Regulations.

This section of the Code of Federal Regulations establishes the set of financial information that companies need to disclose. In other words, it operationalizes the disclosure requirements set up by the SEC Act of 1933.

"Instructions to Item 301:

1. The purpose of the selected financial data shall be to supply in a convenient and readable format selected financial data which highlight certain significant trends in the registrant's financial condition and results of operations.

2. Subject to appropriate variation to conform to the nature of the registrant's business, the following items shall be included in the table of financial data: net sales or operating revenues; income (loss) from continuing operations; income (loss) from continuing operations per common share; total assets; long-term obligations and redeemable preferred stock (including long-term debt, capital leases, and redeemable preferred stock as defined in § 210.5-02.27(a) of Regulation S-X [17 CFR 210]; and cash dividends declared per common share. Registrants may include additional items which they believe

would enhance an understanding of and would highlight other trends in their financial condition and results of operations.

Briefly describe, or cross-reference to a discussion thereof, factors such as accounting changes, business combinations or dispositions of business operations, that materially affect the comparability of the information reflected in selected financial data. Discussion of, or reference to, any material uncertainties should also be included where such matters might cause the data reflected herein not to be indicative of the registrant's future financial condition or results of operations.

3. All references to the registrant in the table of selected financial data and in this Item shall mean the registrant and its subsidiaries consolidated.

4. If interim period financial statements are included, or are required to be included, by Article 3 of Regulation S-X, registrants should consider whether any or all of the selected financial data need to be updated for such interim periods to reflect a material change in the trends indicated; where such updating information is necessary, registrants shall provide the information on a comparative basis unless not necessary to an understanding of such updating information.

5. A foreign private issuer shall disclose also the following information in all filings containing financial statements:

A. In the forepart of the document and as of the latest practicable date, the exchange rate into U.S. currency of the foreign currency in which the financial statements are denominated;

B. A history of exchange rates for the five most recent years and any subsequent interim period for which financial statements are presented setting forth the rates for period end, the average rates, and the range of high and low rates for each year; and

C. If equity securities are being registered, a five year summary of dividends per share stated in both the currency in which the financial statements are denominated and United States currency based on the exchange rates at each respective payment date.

6. A foreign private issuer shall present the selected financial data in the same currency as its financial statements. The issuer may present the selected financial data on the basis of the accounting principles used in its primary financial statements but in such case shall present this data also on the basis of any reconciliations of such data to United States generally accepted accounting principles and Regulation S-X made pursuant to Rule 4-01 of Regulation S-X (§ 210.4-01 of this chapter).

7. For purposes of this rule, the rate of exchange means the noon buying rate in New York City for cable transfers in foreign currencies as certified for customs purposes by the Federal Reserve Bank of New York. The average rate means the average of the exchange rates on the last day of each month during a year."

Blank Crowdfunding Business Slides

- Company Name
- Company Address
- Company Website
- Company Facebook Page
- Company LinkedIn Profile
- Company e-mail
- Company Phone

Summary

2

Tagline

Our Key Asset(s)

Team

3

Track Record

Personnel (subject to change)		
Advisors	Employees	Manager

Problem

4

Solution

5

Marketing

6

Potential Customers:

Market Size:

Customer Acquisition:

Sales

Sales:

Pipeline:

Support:

Competition

Current:	

Our Competitive Advantages:

Conclusion

10

Milestones

9 **Current Status**

Projected Expenses, by quarter	1	2	3	Summary
Salaries				
Managers				
Advisors				
Employees				
Office				
Legal				
Marketing and Promotion				
Other expenses				
Total				

Capital Request

11

Value Analysis

	One-time investment	2012	2013	2014	2015
PROFIT ENHANCEMENT		Increased value of Company			
NET VALUE					
Cumulative total					
ROI (four year)					
IRR					

We are seeking $ by selling equity in (Company Name)

Funds will be used to hire additional personnel, for promoting, and for expanding the company.

Repayment will come from other revenues and an increase in Company's value.

Index

CPSIA information can be obtained at www.ICGtesting.com
Printed in the USA
LVOW05s1822120813

347508LV00001B/2/P